COSMO QUIZ BOOK

COSMO QUIZ BOOK

**Edited by
Barbara Creaturo**

HEARST BOOKS
New York, New York

PICTURE CREDITS: ii—Jacques Silberstein. iv—Klaus Lucka. viii—Barry McKinley, David McCabe. 3—Larry Dale Gordon. 8—Ron Nicolaysen. 13—Dave Cox. 19—Norman Mosallem. 25—Nancy Brown. 30—Dennis Milbauer. 34— Elizabeth Koda-Callan, Jeff Mangiat, from photograph by Mary Ann Reinmiller. 37—Ron Nicolaysen. 43—Dominique Silberstein. 49—Norman Mosallem. 55—Norman Mosallem. 67—George Chinsee. 72—Werner Kappes. 75—Ted Wachs. 81—Norman Mosallem. 86—Howard Zager. 90—Anthony Edgeworth. 95—William Maier. 100—Richard Giglio. 106—Patricia Dryden. 109—Steve Landis. 115—Theo. 120—Steve Landis. 125—Norman Mosallem. 129—Tony Costa. 132—Peter Castellano. 138—Bernard Bonhomme. 141—Peter Vaeth. 145—Jacques Silberstein. 149—Karen Radkai. 153—Rosemary Howard. 156—Ron Nicolaysen. 158—Frank Edwards (Mariette Hartley and Margaret Hamilton); Universal Studios (Murray Hamilton). 161—Dave Cox.

Contents

Introduction

Are you smart about yourself? Honest about your own strengths and weak points? You *should* be! Self-aware people are, I find, not just the happiest but also the best to be *around*. It's only after you've delved *deeply* into your own nature that you're able to manage it—*and* your relationships—with grace and style.

The quizzes assembled here are designed to *sharpen* your understanding of self. Don't think you're not going to have *fun* with these little tests (they are *amusing!*), but I'll bet you come away from them with a more secure idea of *who* you are and of how you can get the most happiness and *good* out of life.

The first subject we've covered here is sex —is there any *doubt* that grappling with this aspect of your nature is *essential?* Quite probably, you love men and are therefore interested in becoming a skilled, caring partner in the bedroom. Well, several of our quizzes "rate" your amorous technique, while disclosing the kind of strokes that most please *you*.

Speaking of strokes, our next (and just as vital) subject is the man in your life. Is he the good, solid, lovely person you *deserve?* Or is he *lacking* in a few *not* such insignificant ways? Possibly your relationship is wonderfully gratifying and harmonious, but maybe you two are having a bit of *trouble?* Read and find *out!*

Personal style is a topic that's always arrested *my* interest, too. And it can alter *your* life. If you're overly-dependent on other people's approval, for example, or not sufficiently assertive (in a healthy, *non*-domineering way), then you've got to muster some resolve and make some changes in your behavior. (On the other hand, if you're an intrepid high-scorer whose strength *never* over-bears, hooray for you!)

Next, we come to emotional depths—how do you *operate* in the world of feelings? How skilled are you in having needs *met?* Don't you want to *know?* Our quizzes measure your maturity and generosity, as well as many *other* intriguing components of your make-up.

Finally, do you ever wonder if maybe you could be a bit *smarter?* A number of these quizzes are designed to gauge *mental* acumen —after taking them you'll know if you need to peel open a few books or newspapers and do some *homework*.

At least, after answering these questions, you'll know whether you are sexy, sharp, kind, gracious, linked up with the right man and *more*. Aren't you eager to find out? Well, pour yourself a soda, sharpen some pencils, and let's *go*. . . .

Helen Gurley Brown

Your Sex Profile

So much has been written about sex in recent years that you'd think we'd all be *over*-informed. Not so! Our needs in this area are so singular, so unique, that even *after* digesting mounds of information, one still wonders—but what about me? Why am I sometimes (or even *always!*) left unsatisfied in bed?

The qualities we are measuring here are quite diverse, yet each of them figures importantly in your sexual happiness. The first is adventurousness—the willingness and ability to *risk* yourself in bed. Without enough experimentation your sex life will be pallid. Too much, though, and you're courting danger!

Sexual normality also needs definition. When does the pleasantly kinky turn into the *perverse*? Find out if your behavior is naughty or *nuts*. What about your level of libidinous energy? Are you drably undersexed? Verging on nymphomania? Or balanced happily somewhere in between? And how smart are you about a man's sexuality? (Keeping him happy means knowing how male equipment *works!*)

Next, you'll find out if your style of loving meshes with *his*. ("Incompatibles" break *up!*) Finally, how good a lover are you *really*? He'll never tell the truth about that one, so try the quiz if you dare find out.

Are You Sexually Adventurous?

ADRIENNE SMALL

Now that you *can* have tremendous sexual freedom if you want to take advantage of it, how well do you respond to the challenge? Are you a little frightened of where experimenting might lead, or do you take foolhardy risks in the quest for erotic variety? Naturally, not every woman *wants* to live on the sexual frontier—but your true adventurous desires may be shackled by unconscious timidity. This quiz will show you how shy or bold you *really* are.

For each of the following situations, choose the response that is *most nearly* like your own.

1. You get into the cab, and the handsome young driver asks you to go home with him. You:
a. Leave the cab and hail another.
b. Tell him to pull over and get into the back seat with you.
c. Say that if he's going off duty, you'll have a drink with him at a nearby bar.
d. Refuse his request but stay in the cab.

2. You and your lover or husband come home from a party at 4:00 A.M., and you suddenly feel like making love standing in the downstairs hall of your small apartment building. You:
a. Suppress the desire—opt for going upstairs to make love *there*.
b. Kiss and caress him until *he* gets the idea.
c. Kiss him, let yourself be turned on by the *fantasy* of making love there, then seductively lead him upstairs.

3. A man you met while walking your dog in the park calls and invites you to dinner at a restaurant. You accept. Then he says, "Please wear black stockings—regular stockings, not pantyhose—and a garter belt." You:
a. Tell him you're not interested in that kind of thing.
b. Ask what *he's* going to wear.
c. Agree, wear the outfit . . . and see what the evening brings.

4. You're about to make love with a man for the first time—in *your* bedroom. You:
a. Turn the light down or off.
b. Leave the light on.
c. Ask which he'd prefer.

5. A girl friend gets locked out of her apartment and must stay over at your place—in your double bed. During the night, she makes an unmistakable pass at you. You:
a. Pretend to be asleep.
b. Tell her you're a confirmed heterosexual.
c. Don't know *how* you'd react: you'd have to actually experience the situation to see if you felt attracted to her or not.

6. At a party, you're wildly attracted to a sensual seventeen-year-old boy, who asks if he can take you home. You:
a. Beckon him into the bedroom at the party, lock the door and let him take it from there.
b. Thank him charmingly and ask him to call you in twenty years.
c. Go home together, ask him in for coffee, and see what happens.

7. You've occasionally had a (sexually exciting) rape fantasy. You:
a. Recall the fantasy while making love; it heightens your pleasure.
b. Think the fantasy reflects an unliberated submissiveness, try to take more of a sexual lead yourself in future lovemaking.
c. Tell your lover or husband about the fantasy, implying that you'd like to act it out in bed.

8. You and your man:
a. Are verbal about sex . . . talk about lovemaking before, during and after sex.
b. Communicate mostly through caresses and a kind of secret (but not specifically sexy) language of your own.
c. Are so tuned into each other you rarely *need* overt sexy communication.

9. You get a 16 mm. movie camera and a projector as a present—what you'd most like to do is:
a. Make a charming film of your lover at the beach and in other settings.
b. Rent a copy of *Deep Throat* and invite him for a private screening.
c. Set the camera on a tripod, make love in front of it, then invite him over again to view the results.

10. Ideally, on a vacation trip to the Yucatán, you'd:
a. Travel with your lover, and enjoy having sex in unfamiliar places.
b. Travel alone or with a friend, have a splendid but unsexy time, and enjoy the erotic renaissance with your man when you return.
c. Travel alone or with a friend and have at least one holiday affair with someone you meet.

11. Which of these most nearly describes your feeling while making love?
a. Floating in a lovely tranquil pool.
b. Swimming in an exhilarating surf.
c. Expertly riding a surf board.

12. You've showered and are already dressed in bra and panties; your lover is in the shower, and asks you to join him. You:
a. Laughingly tell him he's insane, to dry off and come have a drink with you.
b. Take off your clothes and jump in.
c. Jump in leaving your underwear *on.*

13. On the way to the supermarket, you meet an old love and the sparks are rekindled. He asks you to come with him *right then*. Remembering that you haven't shaved your legs or underarms in several days, you:
a. Go with him and secretly use his razor in the bathroom.
b. Go with him and explain, when he looks closely at your body during lovemaking, that you've adopted European customs . . . of all kinds.
c. Make a date to meet him in two hours.

14. You've just introduced your new lover to some close friends. Later they're most likely to tell you:
a. "He's *exactly* your type!"
b. "Where do you *find* them? We never know what to expect from you."
c. "But he's the *fourth* this year and it isn't even spring."

15. A highly satisfactory love affair has ended. You're likely to feel:
a. Disillusioned a little . . . men *do* cause such pain.
b. Sad for having been unable to make the love affair work any longer.
c. Sad but plotting the next adventure.

16. At a party, a staggeringly handsome (and nice) man pays you many attentions. You feel:
a. Flattered, but doubt this could lead to Something Serious.
b. A bit skeptical—he's apt to be a Don Juan.
c. Pleased and drawn to him in return.

17. Someone you're crazy about "dares" you to do something risky (gamble your return air fare at baccarat; streak the police station; dive from a cliff into the Mediterranean). You'd probably:
a. Weigh the dangers carefully before deciding.
b. Say no—no matter what he thinks about you.
c. Rise to the challenge—you are as adventurous as he.

18. Your fantasy sex-city would most likely be:
a. (Kinky) Hamburg.
b. (Romantic) Paris.
c. (Lusty) Rio de Janeiro.

19. Which of the following sex scenarios is most like your own fantasies?
a. At an elegant cocktail party, a man you don't know orders you to take off your clothes and lie down on the floor. He then makes love to you in full view of the other guests.
b. You secretly take a job in an exclusive bordello, and yield to the bizarre tastes of a series of customers.
c. You and your lover have sex on a bed of leaves in an alpine meadow.

20. You would most like to star in a movie directed by:
a. Bernardo Bertolucci.
b. François Truffaut.
c. Robert Altman.

21. A friend tells you she accepted $100 to let a man look at her for ten minutes while she wore nothing but a flower behind one ear. You:
a. Want to know all the details but are somewhat repelled.
b. Find the idea sexually exciting and wish an

attractive man would ask you to do something that far-out.
c. Think that your friend made easy money, but you know *you'd* never have the nerve.

22. When alone, you:
a. Often touch and look at your naked body, and wish someone were there to appreciate it.
b. Rarely glimpse at yourself naked except while undressing or bathing.
c. *Occasionally* examine your naked body in a full-length mirror.

SCORING: Give yourself points as follows. Then add up your score to see how sexually adventurous you are.

1.	a.1	b.3	c.2	d.2	**12.**	a.1	b.2	c.3	
2.	a.1	b.3	c.2		**13.**	a.2	b.3	c.1	
3.	a.1	b.2	c.3		**14.**	a.1	b.3	c.2	
4.	a.1	b.2	c.3		**15.**	a.3	b.1	c.2	
5.	a.1	b.2	c.3		**16.**	a.1	b.2	c.3	
6.	a.3	b.1	c.2		**17.**	a.2	b.1	c.3	
7.	a.2	b.1	c.3		**18.**	a.6	b.2	c.4	
8.	a.3	b.2	c.1		**19.**	a.4	b.6	c.2	
9.	a.1	b.2	c.3		**20.**	a.4	b.2	c.6	
10.	a.1	b.2	c.3		**21.**	a.2	b.6	c.4	
11.	a.2	b.3	c.1		**22.**	a.6	b.2	c.4	

29-44: While not exactly a sexual *hermit* (you wouldn't have been able to *answer* these questions if you were), you may not be taking advantage of the freedom available to women in this post-sexual-revolution age. You're still reluctant to express desire—perhaps fearing the man will think you're too aggressive or needy. As a result, you miss out on marvelous chances to explore your sexuality. You may also tend to have unrealistic expectations of sex, and to be disappointed when lovers aren't perfect cavaliers who know—without being told—exactly what you want. The romantic in you is charming, but can make you timid about discussing sex, trying unfamiliar partners or techniques; you've probably had the same lover or *type* of lover for years.

Men may interpret your reticence as selfishness. You must learn that sexual adventure is not dirty talk and erotic appliances, but an openness to giving and receiving. Try talking *more* about sex—with friends, lovers. Avoid routine: make tiny changes from time to time in the setting where you usually have sex (candles instead of a lamp, special music) to encourage daring and sensuality.

45-69: You're a healthy, liberated woman, unashamedly sexual and able to communicate your desires. However, you're a little confused about what you should be *doing* with all this new freedom. Sometimes you feel *obliged* to vary your sex life; other times, you long for a romantic, true-love commitment. Don't be too buffeted by these emotional shifts—they're natural.

Because your sense of self is secure, you can *handle* sexual adventure. So don't be afraid of new partners and unfamiliar voyages into the erotic unknown; you'll know whether you like them or not, and will be honest enough to say so. Don't let empathy for a man lock you into a relationship you don't truly enjoy; you deserve a deeply sexual man, and he deserves you.

71-87: You're a free spirit who lets very little stand in the way of pleasure pursuits. Your initiative, openness and willingness to try anything once may frighten off *some* men, but that doesn't bother you—there are so many more to know.

Be careful, though, not to let your search for erotic variety get you into trouble. A little self-protection is in order, capricious one! Beware of rushing into bed with any stranger, or of spreading yourself so thin that you never have the chance to luxuriate in a sweetly prolonged affair. Your scorn for romanticism may *deprive* you of some forms of sexual experience—the kind that come with love and tenderness. Try to cultivate some male *friends,* too.

How Normal Are You Sexually?

CAROLE HAY

Even though literally *thousands* of sex surveys have been made and published since the pioneering Kinsey Reports (on such subjects as how you respond to "blue" movies, how many sexual thoughts you have per hour, what your preferred method of intercourse is, etc.) many girls continue to think there's something peculiar about their sexuality, that they're either too repressed and virginal *or* too extravagant and freaky in sexual activities. Some of us never disclose sexual pleasures for fear we'll be labeled outrageous or foolish; meanwhile, friends are enjoying the very same secret delights. Wouldn't you smile if you knew last night's experiment with your lover was common practice? Seductive lady, you may be more normal than you think. Why not take our quiz to find out exactly where you stand!

Answer *all* the following questions, choosing the response that comes closest to your own. If you have trouble deciding between two responses, you may check them both. Don't check *more* than two.

1. At what age were you no longer a virgin?
a. 15 or under
b. 16 to 19
c. 20 to 25
d. Over 25

2. With how many men have you had sex?
a. 1 to 3   **e.** Over 20
b. 4 to 6   **f.** 30 to 50
c. 7 to 10   **g.** Too many to count
d. Over 10

3. How many times a month do you have a sexual experience of any type, including masturbation?
a. 1 to 9   **c.** Over 20
b. 10 to 20   **d.** Daily: once or more than once

4. During intercourse, you experience orgasm:
a. Never
b. Occasionally
c. Most of the time

5. In foreplay, you are most aroused by caresses to:
a. Clitoris
b. Vagina
c. Breasts and nipples
d. Other areas (buttocks, whole body, etc.)
e. Everything

6. What is the greatest amount of orgasms you ever had in one night (or day)?
a. 1 to 3   c. Over 7
b. 4 to 7   d. Over 10

7. How many positions (man on top, you on top, side-by-side, etc.) do you use in intercourse?
a. 1 only   c. 4 to 6
b. 2 to 3   d. More than 6

8. Your preferred position in making love is:
a. Man on top
b. Woman on top
c. From the rear, with you kneeling or lying down
d. Side-by-side, front to front
e. Side-by-side, his front to your back
f. Some other position
g. *All* positions: You like variety

9. Do you ever engage in oral sex (man to woman, woman to man, or both)?
a. Yes, frequently   c. No
b. Yes, occasionally

10. You would describe your sexual drive as:
a. Extremely strong
b. Strong
c. Moderate
d. Rather low
e. Quite low

11. Your reaction to seeing a man in the nude is:
a. Excitement and attraction
b. Gentle aesthetic pleasure
c. Embarrassment or distaste
d. Reaction depends on who it is or how you're feeling at the moment

12. Your reaction to a man seeing *you* in the nude is:
a. Exciting and pleasurable
b. Embarrassing
c. Depends on the man

13. Do you often find it difficult to achieve orgasm by intercourse alone (without additional clitoral, anal, or breast stimulation by him *or* you)?
a. Yes   b. No

14. Do you sometimes fantasize during intercourse (imagining you are someone else, your partner is someone else, that you have an audience, or you're both being filmed for an X-rated movie, etc.)?
a. Yes   b. No

15. In making love, you are the aggressor (taking the initiative):
a. Usually
b. Quite often
c. Sometimes
d. Rarely
e. Never

16. With a new man, you will have intercourse:
a. Immediately, on the first date
b. The second or third time you go out
c. After a suitable introductory period

17. You are most turned on by a man who uses a:
a. Romantic, emotional courtship
b. Quite direct, let's-go-to-bed approach
c. The approach really doesn't matter, it's how well you like the man

18. Being forcefully and aggressively taken by a man:
a. Always appeals to you and turns you on
b. Is occasionally appealing
c. Might appeal as a fantasy, but never in actuality
d. Is threatening or repellent

19. The most men you've ever been to bed with in a twenty-four-hour period is:
a. 1
b. 2
c. 3 to 4
d. 5 or more

20. Do you ever enjoy being spanked or punished during, before, or after the sexual act?
a. Yes, often
b. Occasionally
c. Never

21. Have you ever indulged in sex with more than one person at a time?
a. Yes
b. No

22. You've had a homosexual experience:
a. Yes, fairly often
b. Yes, only once or a few times
c. No, but the idea intrigues you
d. No, the idea repels

23. How often do sexual thoughts of *any* kind (twinges of desire, thoughts of men being attractive and unattractive, sexy feelings about your own body, memories of love episodes, etc.) cross your mind? Think about this; it's not easy to answer.
a. Every few minutes
b. Several times an hour
c. Once or twice an hour
d. A few times every day
e. Seldom

24. Do you enjoy being undressed by your man?
a. Yes
b. No
c. Only on occasion

25. Do you enjoy undressing him?
a. Yes
b. No
c. On occasion

26. You prefer to make love:
a. In bright light
b. In dim light
c. In darkness or semidarkness
d. All of these

27. Does it turn you on to talk to your man during lovemaking?
a. Yes, romantic love talk
b. Yes, obscene "dirty" talk
c. No, prefer silence

28. Do you like to watch yourself making love in a mirror?
a. Yes, often
b. Occasionally
c. Never

29. Do you make love in the nude?
a. Yes
b. No, being nude doesn't appeal to you at all
c. No, wearing *some* clothes seems more sexy

SCORING:

1.	a.8	b.6	c.4	d.2			
2.	a.2	b.4	c.6	d.8	e.10	f.12	g.15
3.	a.2	b.6	c.8	d.12			
4.	a.0	b.4	c.8				
5.	a.6	b.4	c.8	d.10	e.12		
6.	a.4	b.6	c.10	d.15			
7.	a.1	b.4	c.8	d.12			
8.	a.1	b.4	c.12	d.6	e.10	f.12	g.15
9.	a.12	b.8	c.2				
10.	a.12	b.8	c.6	d.4	e.0		
11.	a.12	b.8	c.0	d.6			
12.	a.12	b.2	c.4				
13.	a.4	b.10					
14.	a.12	b.4					
15.	a.10	b.8	c.6	d.4	e.0		
16.	a.15	b.10	c.4				
17.	a.6	b.15	c.10				
18.	a.15	b.8	c.4	d.0			
19.	a.4	b.8	c.12	d.15			
20.	a.15	b.8	c.2				
21.	a.15	b.2					
22.	a.15	b.10	c.8	d.2			
23.	a.10	b.6	c.4	d.2	e.0		
24.	a.10	b.2	c.6				
25.	a.12	b.4	c.8				
26.	a.12	b.8	c.4	d.15			
27.	a.6	b.12	c.4				
28.	a.15	b.8	c.4				
29.	a.6	b.2	c.12				

Scoring instructions: Add up the points for your answers. If you checked *two* answers to any question, add the two point scores then divide by two to get your score. (Example: You checked a [6 points] and c [10 points]: 6 + 10 = 16. Half of 16, or 8, is your score.)

If you are under sixteen, add *50 points* to your total score. Seventeen to nineteen: add *20 points*. Other age groups use the point total unchanged. It doesn't make any difference whether you're married or single; this quiz is designed to apply to both groups. A wife usually has opportunities for greater frequency of intercourse, but the single girl potentially has a wider variety of partners, so the two factors balance each other out.

WHAT YOUR SCORE MEANS

Above 290: You are definitely oversexed, perhaps compulsive in your activities. Marriage, or any other one-to-one relationship, would be rather difficult for you to maintain because of your semi-insatiable desire for new experiences and partners.

246-290: This is the upper normal range. Your sexual responses are positive and enthusiastic. You want and need more sex than the average person, and require a man whose drives are similar. It's *torture* for you to be with a cold or sexually apathetic lover. When you find the right man, you can be extremely loyal, but the partnership might be unconventional —it's unusual for someone with drives as strong as yours to be completely a "one-man woman."

161-245: This is the most "normal" point range. Sex is not an overwhelming preoccupation for you, but you do think of it as a basic and happy part of your life, something to be enjoyed and welcomed. If married, it's probable you've been unfaithful to your husband once or twice, or will be within the next few years. You may also have had one or two rather far-out sexual experiences. With your regular partner you indulge in a variety of positions and practices that would have shocked Grandma or Great-aunt Martha. Nevertheless, your sexual attitudes and preferences are typical of the average young American woman today.

120-160: The lower normal range. This score indicates that sex does not figure very prominently in your life. Perhaps a religious upbringing inclines you to be somewhat more strait-laced than the average. Or you may be in a marriage where the sexual fires have cooled. Possibly you are simply not very highly sexed—millions of women are not and do not necessarily suffer.

Below 120: This would indicate a considerable degree of sexual apathy and resignation, or at least a very low sex drive. Someone with this score would probably be a great deal happier as a spinster than in a sexual relationship of any kind.

How High Is Your Sexual-Energy Level?

CAROLE HAY

Sexual energy (Freud called it libido) is mysterious and so *powerful*. Whether you enjoy, control, or repress feelings in the bedroom—and how subtly or vigorously—influences your total approach to life. Some girls prowl and romp like tigresses, others have delicate flames that need continual nurturing, and many are seemingly quiet yet burn with the physical power of a hundred suns. What's *your* degree of energy? And how do you express mysterious sexual forces? Take our quiz and find out! (Warning: Questions here are often subtle and indirect, so don't try to guess what they mean—just try to answer honestly.)

In each of the following questions, choose the response or responses (some invite more than one) most nearly like your own.

1. A lover takes you to the jewelry store to buy you a gift. You'd choose:
a. A ring with a tiny, exquisite diamond
b. Love bracelets with locks, for two—and give him the key to yours
c. A thin gold chain to drape low around your waist and be seen mostly by him
d. A garnet or amethyst pendant that strategically hangs between your breasts

2. Your dreams while asleep often involve (check as many as apply):
a. Scary, nightmare scenes
b. Vivid yet lyrical erotic encounters
c. Thrilling escapades in which you're pursued but finally escape
d. Lurid visions of rape, humiliation, and punishment
e. Ordinary, life-like situations
f. Orgies or other explicitly sexy scenes
g. Mysterious, haunting visions—you wander endlessly through a strange town or building
h. Sexual escapades with people you *know*
i. Beautiful and peacefully sensuous sequences
j. Action scenes, with you flying or falling
k. Baroque "epics" in which you're a loved and admired heroine

3. Men who attract you are (check as many traits as *stir* you):
a. Tall with classic features
b. Rich
c. Odd-looking in a cute, endearing way
d. Athletic and powerfully built
e. Impeccably suave and sophisticated
f. Brooding and emotional—touched by tragedy or despair
g. Extremely competent and successful
h. Witty and amusing
i. Unpredictable, scary, and sinister
j. Easygoing and well-adjusted
k. Fiercely competitive and ambitious
l. Deliciously evil and decadent

4. Thinking about your breasts makes you (check just one):
a. Grow depressed—Raquel Welch you're not
b. Feel happy and glad you're a woman
c. Want to call up your lover
d. Stand up straight

5. To you, dirty jokes are (check one):
a. A turn-on—amusing *and* sexy
b. A turn-off because most are so crude
c. Fine when they're *funny*
d. Humor you accept only because men enjoy telling them

6. Cast as the heroine of a rousing, old-time melodrama, you'd prefer to be the girl who:
a. Is sold into slavery and becomes the love-plaything of a sheik
b. Is fought over by two knights at King Arthur's court . . . they joust to the death to win your favor
c. Gets marooned on a lush island with a cool-headed ship's officer
d. Falls sweetly asleep in the forest and is ravished by a swarthy young peasant

7. Usually you feel menstruation is:
a. Reassuring confirmation of your woman-hood
b. A welcome arrival—you've survived, un-pregnant, for another month
c. You don't think much about it
d. A bother, quite unfair

8. Which of the following make you feel sexy? Check as many as you wish:
a. Being whistled at by construction workers, truck drivers
b. Sitting on a lush velvet sofa
c. Having dinner with a man in a candlelit restaurant or in your own apartment
d. Reading or viewing a pornographic book or movie
e. Watching a *violent* movie
f. Reading a lovely but sad, romantic novel
g. Receiving suggestive flattery from a charming foreigner
h. Direct sexual invitations
i. Stares from a stranger across a room
j. All-out praise of your breasts, backside, pelvis, etc.

9. Watching far-out nude love scenes in an X-rated movie makes you feel:
a. Horny and eager to try some of the positions yourself
b. Titillated but a little smarmy and, well, *unclean*
c. Ambivalent—you enjoy seeing good-looking bodies but the sex seems too contrived, freaky, or unnatural
d. Amused but unaroused

10. Which of these foods are sexily appealing? Check as many as tempt you:
a. Champagne and caviar
b. A huge rare steak

c. Lobster dripping with butter
d. Flaming cherries jubilee
e. Steak tartare and raw oysters
f. Breast of guinea hen under glass
g. Corn on the cob
h. Ripe Brie or Camembert
i. Huge slice of icy watermelon
j. Big, gloriously ripe peaches

11. You're getting married and a wealthy aunt will give the honeymoon trip as a gift. You'd choose a:
a. Luxury hotel in a beautiful tropical resort
b. Rustic cabin—very secluded, so he'll have nothing to do but pay attention to you
c. Thirty-day tour of Europe
d. Schooner cruise of the Caribbean

12. You're aware, of course, how weather and atmosphere can influence moods and heighten experience. Which of these environments make *you* sexy? Check as many as you wish:
a. Darkness
b. Rainy or misty afternoons
c. Bright sun and blooming wildflowers
d. Sudden thunderstorms
e. Icicles and snowdrifts
f. Bracing fall winds
g. Sand and surf
h. Moonlight
i. Balmy spring air

13. The idea of not shaving under your arms strikes you as:
a. Sexy—a turn-on
b. Mildly disgusting
c. Acceptable and natural, but not especially sexual
d. Too untidy for you

14. Wearing a truly elegant mink coat, you'd most enjoy:
a. The feel of it against your naked body
b. Making love on the soft fur
c. Showing the quality off to someone who knows fur
d. The way *you* look wrapped up in it

15. You think making love would be exciting in (check all the places that intrigue you):
a. An elegant penthouse
b. The back of a pick-up truck
c. A rock star's private Lear jet
d. An elevator stopped between floors
e. A sauna
f. A 747 late at night
g. An artist's loft
h. A balcony, within earshot of the neighbors
i. The back room of a hardware store
j. A cemetery
k. The laundromat
l. A public room of the White House
m. The back row at the movies
n. Your parents' living room
o. Your own bedroom
p. A terrace overlooking the Bay of Capri
q. A tent in Africa, while on safari
r. The basement of your apartment building

16. After not making love for a long period you:
a. Fantasize wildly
b. Grow anxious and jumpy
c. Feel *every* emotion more intensely
d. It would never happen—you manage to satisfy yourself no matter where you are

17. A tempting sexual experiment would be (check more than one, if you wish):
a. Going to an orgy
b. A lesbian relationship

c. Taking a lover much older or younger than you are
d. Many lovers all at once
e. Posing for a *Playboy* centerfold
f. Wearing exotic underwear for your lover
g. Seducing your doctor
h. Answering the doorbell nude

18. If you were without a man and feeling horny, you'd be most apt to:
a. Stimulate yourself
b. Impulsively seduce a new lover
c. Play tennis or go jogging to take your mind off sex
d. Take initiative with a dear man *friend*

19. How do you regard girls who blush a lot? Choose the statement closest to your opinion:
a. They're shy and immature
b. They're inhibited but would like to break loose
c. Blushing has no real significance; some people just naturally get red in the face easily
d. Their sexual feelings are probably *explosive*

20. Who, among the following men, do you find sexy? Check any number:
a. John Travolta
b. Telly Savalas
c. John Ritter
d. Clint Eastwood
e. Peter Falk
f. Yul Brynner
g. Woody Allen
h. Paul Newman
i. Burt Reynolds
j. Omar Sharif
k. Robert Redford
l. Johnny Carson

SCORING: Record your letter scores in one column, your number totals for questions 2, 3, 8, 10, 12, 15, 17, and 20 in another.

1. a.Z b.X c.W d.Y
2. Give yourself 1 point for each reply checked.
3. One point for each reply.
4. a.Z b.Y c.X d.W
5. a.W b.Z c.Y d.X
6. a.W b.X c.Z d.Y
7. a.Y b.Z c.W d.X
8. One point for each reply.
9. a.W b.X c.Y d.Z
10. One point for each reply.
11. a.X b.W c.Z d.Y
12. One point for each reply.
13. a.W b.X c.Y d.Z
14. a.Y b.W c.Z d.X
15. One point for each reply.
16. a.Z b.Y c.X d.W
17. One point for each reply.
18. a.Y b.W c.Z d.X
19. a.Z b.Y c.W d.X
20. One point for each reply.

Questions with lettered response indicate your *style* of sexuality (more about that later). The total score for questions 2, 3, 8, 10, 12, 15, 17, and 20 reveals your *degree* of sexual energy:

More than 55: Ultrahigh. Your supercharged libido gives you awesome life-affirming zest. When in a good mood (as you are *usually*) you like, even love, people and crave a ceaseless stream of adventurous experiences! Probably you're extremely creative or artistic—your strength of mind and spirit demand that imaginative thoughts be realized. Whether a classic-boned beauty or a gamine charmer, you've an inner spunkiness that even critical rivals admire. Because your love style is invariably so passionate, though, emotions easily turn stormy when you feel crossed or slighted. You're apt to have many lovers at a time and break off unpromising relationships quickly. Frail men shy away—you're too powerful a force to be trifled with!

31 to 55: High. Your sexuality is an energizing force that enhances *every* aspect of your life. Clear-eyed and direct, your quiet competence and easy confidence result from being in *touch* with basic sexual instincts. Though you take pleasure in feeling womanly and are *deeply* sexy, you don't necessarily make an effort to dress that way, and first-time lovers are apt to be astounded by the intensity of your lovemaking. Unlike more flamboyant girls, you're easily compatible with many different types of men (macho, very sensitive, *or* timid). Your passions, while strong, smolder steadily and give off amazing warmth.

16 to 30: Medium. Your energy level is *typical* of most girls (men, too); still, this relatively modest point total doesn't mean you *can't* be as fiery or sexually active as high-rated types. You'll simply have to *work* at achieving peak experiences for awhile. Initially you may need to "psych" yourself by fantasizing, or risk a few bolder-than-usual encounters. Your strong point: Medium energy girls naturally choose mates and sex partners carefully and if you *use* innate discretion to select adventurous (energizing) lovers, you can expect much wildfire!

15 points or less: Low energy. You're a romantic, rather fragile creature who, nevertheless, relies rather heavily on nerve and willpower to get through life. Don't you want to become a *little* more of a hedonist? An innately frail nature can be overcome if you draw on spiritual instead of physical energies. Ethereal women (your type tends to have more *intensity* than stamina) *can* reach passionate highs with a lover who complements their *total* emotional nature. Careful *who* you choose, though—with a pallid man, your own fires stay banked!

HOW YOU USE YOUR ENERGIES
Questions graded with letters determine your sexual personality. Check the letter you marked most often to discover how you *use* your libido. If answers are spread among letters almost equally, then your sexual personality is a blend of those types.

W—Tigress. Sex is marvelous adventure to you—sport, art, game, and even, perhaps, your *mission* in life. Ever ready to embrace the new, you glory in your sexuality and emanate an explicit irresistible appeal. And you are willing to *pursue* satisfaction vigorously. No man you've bedded will ever forget you, but very insecure men may find you, well, scary.

X—Romantic. Sex manuals of the clinical, how-to variety are worthless to you. Gentle looks and caresses, tender words, physical closeness—for a night or forever—are what turn *you* on. Earth-bound males might think you dreamy and unsensual, but to the sensitive lover who succeeds in arousing your lusty side, you can be as physical and passionate as the Tigress.

Y—Sybarite. You delight in the pleasures of the body—all of them. Soft breezes on your body, the smell of wildflowers, a sumptuous meal . . . these are almost as appealing to you as the sexual act itself. You take lovers easily and joyfully, and why not? They're part of the great feast of life.

Z—Woman of the World. You have an unerring sense of proportion in everything, including love affairs. Though you find sex delightful, you never let passion divert you totally from practicalities. Not for you the primitive, wildly unappropriate lover who thrills you in bed but nowhere else; the wistful but romantic loser who takes you out on *your* money; or any other eccentric or second-rate man. A thoroughbred yourself, you'll look for the man who's polished, wealthy, intelligent, *and* a good lover . . . why settle for less?

How Well Do You Know Male Sexuality?

JUNIUS ADAMS

Wonderful, well-informed person that you are, you've read *The Joy of Sex, Beyond the Male Myth,* and other enlightening books. You know a lot about your man and his all-important sexual/reproductive equipment—but are you aware of how it all *works?* Take our quiz and find out—you may learn facts that will make sex even more rewarding! (Not to worry if you turn out to be just a *trifle* ignorant about male anatomy—many men are, too!)

1. Semen is produced in:
a. The testicles
b. The prostate gland
c. Both places

2. In each normal ejaculation, there are approximately:
a. 5,000 individual sperm
b. 50,000
c. 10 million
d. 100 million

3. Is a single sperm enough to fertilize the ovum?
Yes _____   No _____

4. In impregnation, does the sperm reach the ovum solely under its own power?
Yes _____   No _____

5. Hardy, long-lived sperm cells tend to produce:
a. Boys   **b.** Girls   **c.** Twins

6. Ejaculation occurs:
a. At the moment of climax
b. Afterward

7. The quantity of semen in an ejaculation will be greater if there has been prolonged foreplay before orgasm.
True _____   False _____

8. The temperature within the testicles is:
a. The same as the rest of the body's
b. Two degrees cooler
c. Two degrees warmer

9. The penis is the most delicate, sensitive part of a man's sexual equipment.
True ____
False ____

10. For most males, erections begin:
a. Almost at birth
b. Around age eight or nine
c. At puberty—twelve to fifteen

11. Men continue to have erections:
a. All their lives
b. Until their sixties or seventies
c. For varying periods—individuals differ

12. Is the penis under conscious control—can a man "will" himself to have an erection?
Yes ____   No ____

13. At what age is a man biologically most "potent" in number and strength of possible ejaculations?
a. Twenty-three to thirty
b. Thirty to forty-five
c. Thirteen to twenty-two
d. Over forty-five

14. Do adolescents and younger males have more "erect" erections than older men?
Yes ____   No ____

15. The man best equipped to handle "exotic" or far-out sexual positions generally belongs to which age group?
a. Over thirty
b. Under thirty

16. Impotence is usually caused by:
a. Psychological factors
b. Physical weakness or disease
c. A combination of both

17. With advancing years, men tend to:
a. Lose their sexual drive, partly or completely
b. Retain desire, but not capacity
c. Retain both desire and capacity

18. Unlike women, men do not have monthly "cycles."
True ____
False ____

19. Men have fewer erogenous zones than women.
True ____
False ____

20. A man is fully aroused and ready for sex as soon as he has achieved erection.
True ____
False ____

21. Men are capable of only *one* kind of orgasm.
True ____
False ____

22. Men in good physical condition have more pleasurable orgasms than those who are out of shape.
True ____
False ____

23. Men tend to have fuller, more satisfactory orgasms through:
a. Sex with a partner
b. Masturbation

24. Men are less able to tolerate sexual frustration than women.

True ____

False ____

25. Impotent men have no feeling in their genital organs.

True ____

False ____

26. "Rape" of a man by a woman is an anatomical impossibility.

True ____

False ____

ANSWERS

1. c. Both places. Sperm cells, or spermatozoon, are produced within the testes, while the fluid in which they travel comes from the prostate gland. Both (together they are known as semen) are released into the ejaculatory duct at the moment of orgasm.

2. d. 100 million. An incredible number, yes, but nature is profligate about propagation. More than 99 percent of these sperm will perish (due to the acidity of the vagina) long before they reach the Fallopian tubes, where the egg can be fertilized. A man with a sperm count of fewer than 20 million will generally be infertile.

3. No. Although only one sperm actually fertilizes the ovum, the cooperation of thousands is necessary. Sperm are much smaller and frailer than the ovum, and before one can penetrate an egg, a vast number must release a chemical called hyaluronidase, which weakens the egg's outer, protective layer.

4. No. While sperm do "swim" upward toward the ovum, the tiny, hairlike, constantly moving cilia in the Fallopian tubes help speed them on their way.

5. b. Long-lived "survivor" sperm, studies have shown, tend to produce girls, while boys are made by speedy "first arrivals." If a couple wants a girl, then, they should plan to have intercourse two or three days before ovulation; for a boy, *on* the day of ovulation.

6. b. Afterward. At the precise moment of orgasm, semen is released into the ejaculatory duct. From there, however, it must travel the length of the penis before emerging from the urethra. In adolescents and younger men, ejaculation takes place almost immediately and with explosive force. In older men, the journey is more leisurely and may take two or three seconds to complete.

7. True. The longer the male has been stimulated (short of orgasm) before intercourse, the more prostate fluid, and thus ejaculate, will be produced.

8. b. Two degrees cooler. This slight difference in temperature is vital to the health of the sperm. Men whose testicles have not descended (and therefore remain at 98.6 degrees) cannot produce live sperm.

9. False. A man's *testicles* are the most sensitive part of his sexual equipment—any tap, glancing blow, or slight pressure to this area can result in acute pain. (In love-making, testicles can be stroked or cupped in hand or mouth but should never be squeezed or shaken.) The penis, on the other hand, is built to take considerable stress. It can tolerate extremes of heat and cold more easily than almost any other part of a man's body and will also tolerate—even be *stimulated* by—very rough handling, short of being bent in two while erect (which might damage the inner blood-receptor cavities that cause erection). This is not to say, however, that the penis can't respond to *gentle* stimulation as well; though its nerves are concentrated deep within the shaft, numerous nerve fibers run to the surface. The most sensitive spot on the penis is the area within the V-shaped cleft on the underside of the head, or glans.

10. a. Even tiny babies experience erections. By the age of eight or nine, most boys can sustain an erection long enough to permit masturbation or even intercourse, though full potency doesn't occur until puberty.

11. a. Studies show that *all* men, with the exception of those whose impotence is due to physical causes such as cirrhosis of the liver, diabetes, and prostectomy (surgical removal of the prostate gland), have erections during the REM (rapid-eye-movement) stage of sleep. This includes the elderly.

12. Either answer is correct. Lust, arousal, and the urge to erection all take place in the deeper, more instinctive reaches of the mind and are not amenable to conscious control. Some control is possible indirectly, however. A man can achieve erection by fantasizing (or looking at or touching) something that appeals to the lustful part of his subconscious or, conversely, get rid of an erection by thinking of (looking at, touching) something *un*appealing. In most cases, a sex partner can rouse a man to erection much more easily than he can rouse himself. The only direct control a man has over his penis is the ability to wiggle it slightly by contracting the erector muscles in his lower abdomen.

13. c. Thirteen to twenty-two. This early potency is probably what inspired the French saying *Si la jeunesse savait, si la vieillesse pouvait* . . . ("If youth only knew; if age only could").

14. Yes—in boys and young men, the erector muscles are extremely tight and hold the penis very high, almost parallel to the body. As a man gets older, however, these muscles loosen their grip, lifting the penis only halfway or a little more than halfway up.

15. a. Men over thirty. For a young man, with his tight erector muscles, positions which pull the penis down from the abdomen or off at an angle—in other words, away from its normal upright stance—can be quite painful.

16. a. According to experts, at least 70 percent of impotence results from anxiety, repressed anger, and various emotional conflicts.

17. c. Though studies show that men tend to make love with slightly less frequency as they grow older, they will retain their desire and capacity for sex as long as suitable partners are available. Sex is no different from any other physical capacity: A vigorous old man can be expected to make love vigorously; a feeble one . . . *feebly*.

18. False—at least for *married* men, who, according to studies, go through the same monthly cycle of mood change and temperature variation as do their wives—no one is *sure* why. What about a married man who sleeps with his wife but has sex only with his mistress? He will "cycle" with the *wife*, say researchers.

19. False. There is more variation *within* the sexes than between them. Some people report dozens of erogenous zones on their body; others mention only one or two. (Yes, quite a few men enjoy having their nipples caressed, and at least some women do *not*.)

20. False. Just because the man is physically ready doesn't mean he's emotionally primed. Often he needs as much as or more foreplay than the woman before his *passions* are raised, so don't assume you have to rush things once he has an erection.

21. False. Many men report having "minor climaxes"—mini-orgasms *without* ejaculations—before and after the main orgasm. According to homosexuals who practice anal intercourse, men may also experience rectal or "prostate" orgasms similar to those experienced by the female during intercourse.

22. True. More than women, men tend to feel orgasm in their muscles, and to feel it more strongly when the muscles are in good condition.

23. b. Masturbation. Although they certainly didn't claim to prefer solitary sex to sex *à deux*, a majority of men queried in one survey said the climaxes they achieved through masturbation were more dependable and physically satisfying than those with a partner.

24. True. Most sex authorities indicate that men experience a more urgent and *physical* drive for sexual satisfaction than do women.

25. False. Sufferers from psychologically based impotence say they have very *strong* feelings in the genital area—which, however, they're unable to satisfy through intercourse. (They *can* masturbate, usually, but cannot sustain an erection with a partner.)

26. False. Men *can* be roused to erection against their (conscious) will and subsequently "taken" by a woman.

SCORING: Give yourself 5 points for each correct answer.

100 to 130: Extraordinary—you know more about men than most of *them* do. You must be a sensational lover!

60 to 95: Yes, you made a few wrong choices —but also enough right ones to show that you *care* . . .

Under 60: Your lack of knowledge could get you into trouble some day! Why not ask your librarian for a good sex manual or, better yet, find a man and get *him* to explain things.

Do Your Love Styles Mesh?

LAURENCE SCHWAB AND KAREN MARKHAM

This test is designed to assess your basic nature—and his—and thus to reveal whether you're romantically compatible. You should find the questions easy enough to answer for both of you—if you know the man well enough! Or, you can ask him to take the test himself. If you're uncertain whether to check a, b, or c on any particular question, simply skip to the next one. It's more important to give accurate replies than to answer every question.

1. Posture   *yours* _____ *his* _____
a. Relaxed.
b. Tense, ready to spring.
c. Reined in, restricted.

2. Movements   *yours* _____ *his* _____
a. Slow, smooth, and flowing.
b. Unhesitant, brisk, and determined.
c. Noiseless, unobtrusive. In the room, without anyone's knowing it.

3. Breathing   *yours* _____ *his* _____
a. Slow, deep, and regular.
b. Fast, deep, and often uneven.
c. Shallow, relatively rapid.

4. Physical surroundings *yours* _____ *his* _____
a. Relishes comfort and, given the choice, will usually pick the softest chair in the room.
b. Requires open spaces with lots of air and water.
c. Prefers snug little nooks and enclosed "cozy spaces."

5. Reactions   *yours* _____ *his* _____
a. Slow and sensuous—never impulsive. Sometimes hard to get moving.
b. Direct, brash. Clumsy at times, but great to have around in emergencies.
c. Graceful and hair-trigger quick.

6. Sex *yours* ___ *his* ___
a. Calm and slow to arouse. Must have affection. Needs right setting. Indefatigable kisser.
b. Has powerful drive and ready anytime, anyplace. Often unaware of partner's needs, but usually a satisfying lover anyway.
c. Easily stimulated, and highly sensitive to partner's needs. But quiet atmosphere is a must!

7. Food *yours* ___ *his* ___
a. Considers eating not just an agreeable ritual, but a way of life.
b. Unfancy tastes. Likes a lot of food, all the time.
c. Something of a gourmet. Often picky. Rejects roughage and fat.

8. Elimination *yours* ___ *his* ___
a. Wastes flow smoothly at regular, scheduled times.
b. Has good elimination. Does not care when, where, or who is around.
c. Often constipated. Must have privacy. Would travel miles to find a clean restroom.

9. Sociability *yours* ___ *his* ___
a. Gregarious. Needs to feel a part of every group. Loves parties.
b. Enjoys competition and must win. Has to be leader. Loves to be a center of attraction.
c. Something of a loner. Has difficulty making party small talk. Prefers reading to relating.

10. Business *yours* ___ *his* ___
a. Likes the red tape of business and is adept at "deals." Works hard at being a company man.
b. Aggressive. Works extremely hard at making projects work—but only when he or she can be boss.
c. Quietly determined, believes thoroughly in his own ideas. Won't go along with the group and occasionally loses out as a result.

11. Sleep *yours* ___ *his* ___
a. Goes to sleep quickly, deeply, and often.
b. Dozes off, but doesn't require much sleep.
c. Insomnia victim. Rises often to check the world. Makes a great human watchdog.

12. Communication *yours* ___ *his* ___
a. Gracious, open and sincere— almost childlike in expressing joy or sorrow.
b. Blunt. Honest. Often brutally so.
c. Rational and unemotional—tries hard to be objective and often succeeds.

13. Voice *yours* ___ *his* ___
a. Well-modulated. Soothing. Children love to listen to his stories.
b. Loud. Brash. Dictatorial. Children obey without question.
c. Quiet, rarely raises voice. Children often say, "But I didn't *hear* you."

14. Feelings about death *yours* ___ *his* ___
a. "Let's not think about that!"
b. Doesn't fear death, but clings tenaciously to life.
c. Anticipates, contemplates, and looks forward to life after death as another new experience.

15. Pain threshold *yours* ___ *his* ___
a. Says ouch before it hurts. Fear of pain more painful than pain itself.
b. Doesn't feel pain until it's almost too late.
c. Hypersensitive to pain. Could easily be a hypochondriac.

16. Appearance   *yours* _____ *his* _____
a. Vital, healthy, unwrinkled.
b. Full of "character"—mature. Often appears older than years.
c. Youthful. People usually underguess this type's age by a decade or so.

17. Alcohol tolerance   *yours* _____ *his* _____
a. Affectionate and gay when drinking.
b. Tends to become boisterous and a bit of a bully.
c. Often melancholy when drunk. Inclined to sulk quietly in corners.

18. Response to trouble   *yours* _____ *his* _____
a. Wants to discuss it at length.
b. Goes right into action. Demands an immediate solution.
c. Likes to be alone to "think things through."

19. Approach to life   *yours* _____ *his* _____
a. What matters is the "here and now."
b. Not afraid of a thing. An adventuresome gambler.
c. Philosophical. Considers life a lesson to be learned.

20. Health   *yours* _____ *his* _____
a. Disgustingly healthy. Couldn't catch a cold in a snowstorm.
b. Rarely sick, hard to keep down when he is.
c. Always suffering from one illness or another—or *imagining* he is.

21. Job preference   *yours* _____ *his* _____
a. Journalism, nursing, public relations, social work—any position that calls for elaborate, ritualistic communication with the public.
b. Construction worker, athlete, salesperson, executive—anything that entails vigorous activity.
c. Enjoys research, scientific studies, and solitary creative pursuits.

22. Bone structure   *yours* _____ *his* _____
a. A large frame covered by fatty tissue.
b. Big, heavy, layered over with muscle.
c. Angular, aquiline, delicate.

23. Nerves   *yours* _____ *his* _____
a. Far beneath the protective fatty tissue. *Nothing* gets to him.
b. Nearer the surface but protected by much muscle. Things seldom get on a "B's" nerves.
c. Right on the surface, so that he's liable to be upset by traffic, airplanes, children. Alert to what's going on around him, however. ESP, occult religious experiences abound in a "C."

SCORING: First, count up the number of a's, b's and c's you checked for yourself. Whichever letter you checked *most* of represents your dominant characteristics. The other letters represent secondary characteristics—disregard a letter entirely if you checked it less than three times. For example, if you checked mostly a's, plus four b's and one c, you would read the "a" section, describing your dominant type, then the section called "Mostly a, some b." Follow the same scoring procedure for your lover. Comparing both your results, you will get a picture of your respective natures and of how romantically well-matched they are.

Mostly A: If a woman, you like to imagine yourself relaxing on a luxurious, satin-pillowed couch. Attentive and comely servants would ply you with nectar and ambrosia while large feathered fans rhythmically stir the sweet-smelling air. Men of this type dream of a large rambling house complete with all the latest luxury appliances and, of course, an oversize water bed. You consider sex a pastime to be leisurely and thoroughly enjoyed, rather like a seven-course meal. No section of the body is taboo. When with the right partner, you're capable of forgetting time completely—and "lost weekends" are common with you. An "A" needs a lover as fond of kissing and caressing as he is. Endurance and plenty of time are a must. Another "A" is the right lover for you, but certain sturdy "B's" are fine too—for a while. Stay away from the wiry "C's" (if indeed you're ever *attracted* to one). Your sybaritic nature would just upset them.

Mostly B: If you're a woman, nothing would please you more than arriving at a political event on the arm of the leading candidate—you'd *adore* the envy of the other women. A man, you'd be pleased to find yourself a gridiron star with many glamorous women in love with you. Impatient, highly sexed and a true conqueror of the world, you know exactly what you want and when you want it. The *perfect* lover for you is another basic "B" who, like you, would never hesitate to ask for what he wants. Though you may get along with the more ritual-loving "A's," they can easily bore you with their lack of drive. And at all costs, avoid the "C" type, who would keep you in a constant rage—in and out of bed.

Mostly C: Your dream of paradise would be yourself snuggled up all warm and safe in some snowbound mountain cabin (with all the conveniences of running water, heat, and a turn-off-able telephone, of course). The "C" type demands complete privacy during the sex act. Children around the house will distract you, as your sensitive nature picks up every sound. A person who is incapable of intelligent conversation or who is *too* emotional would leave you cold, even if he or she is talented in bed. You require a lover who is intellectual and who doesn't demand sex too often. In other words, a "C" type just like you! Stay away from brassy "B" types except for the occasional fling. And the deeply sensual "A's" are *out*. They never get to doing things fast enough for you.

Mostly A, some B: You're a vital, pleasure-loving person, and may just frighten off a prospective sex partner with your need to get things done, now. Further, though outgoing and aggressive, you have a deep fear of being rejected. Don't let that fear hamper you in asking for the sexual gratification you deserve. Pick an even-tempered lover as hedonistic as you are.

Mostly A, some C: You may find you don't enjoy sex as much as you'd like—because you have a tendency to let your *brain* get in the way! Try thinking only about the physical thrill at hand. Stay away from those "B's" who are pushy, dictatorial, and selfish. The perfect lover for you is the predominantly "A" type who dotes on physical pleasure, but is thoughtful enough to appreciate the joys of the intellect as well.

Mostly A, some B and C: Your sense of sexual pleasure allows you to relate well to almost *any* bedmate. Best, however, is the lover who enjoys planning ceremonial love-making complete with the appropriate aphrodisiac.

Mostly B, some A: You're headstrong and courageous—and often willing to take chances in your sex life that another person wouldn't. You prefer warmth to experience in a lover, for you feel that any experience necessary should come from *you*. Avoid "C's" who won't share your desire for sensuality and may be shocked by some of your sexual demands.

Mostly B, some C: Your lust for power drives you to the top, while your intellect and sensitivity give you the cunning to *stay* there. At times you can be brutal and cold, however, so you need a lover who is emotionally secure enough to handle your changes of mood.

Mostly B, some A and C: A lover with any inhibitions would quickly *frustrate* you, and you're alarmed by people who crave the security of marriage. What *you* need is the freedom to roam and experience *all* kinds of lovers. Someone clever, with a zest for fleshly fun would be just right.

Mostly C, some A: You often seem to be two people—one who participates in the sex act, and the other who just watches. You enjoy a romantic lover who whispers endearments while you're making love. Look for the "A" type who takes crises calmly and wouldn't be upset even if you should suddenly up and leave. By all means avoid the "B": Leave *him* and he might come after you—with a *weapon!*

Mostly C, some B: You've a tendency to let your brain rule your genitals, so that you often enjoy talking about sex more than *doing* it! Look for a lover similarly interested. You're too impatient for the plodding "A": his phlegmatic disposition would leave you tapping your foot with impatience.

Mostly C, some A and B: Well-rounded in your sexual interests, you're nevertheless moody—with spurts of enthusiasm one moment and doldrums the next. You need a lover who won't be confused by your sudden switches.

Are You A Good Lover?

ABBY ADAMS

Sure, you're well-groomed and attractive, but are you also the kind of girl a man never forgets . . . or do you perhaps need to *improve* your attitudes and techniques so that you can both get more out of making love? Take our test and find out. Check one answer to each question: either the statement with which you agree the *most*—or the one with which you disagree *least*. Do not pick the answer you *think* is sexiest; give your honest reaction! A scoring section (and an analysis of your lovemaking talents) is at the end of the quiz. Don't peek!

1. How often are *you* the one who initiates lovemaking?
a. Never. You're a man's woman and feel men prefer feminine, nonaggressive girls in bed.
b. Occasionally.
c. Often.
d. Always or almost always.

2. After lovemaking you usually . . .
a. Kiss your lover and tell him he was wonderful.
b. Tell him you have something delicious for him to eat.
c. Kiss your lover and fall asleep.
d. Start talking about things that interest you both that you couldn't get to before lovemaking.

3. You've just finished making love but have not been satisfied. You would . . .

a. Pretend everything is fine (provided you didn't have this problem too often).
b. Tell your lover you're a bit dissatisfied.
c. Be rather quiet and uncommunicative so he could read the secret signs and take steps to make things right.
d. Say nothing but after a few minutes be very loving and attempt to arouse him again.

4. Your lover lets you know he isn't feeling amorous tonight. You . . .
a. Attempt to seduce him by kissing and caressing him.
b. Plan other activities for the evening.
c. Try to get him to talk about why he's not feeling responsive.
d. Without actually touching him behave seductively and let him know you're available should he change his mind.

5. He's questioning you about *former* lovers. You would . . .
a. Skillfully and lovingly change the subject.
b. Tell him everything he wants to know . . . you two are *honest* with each other.
c. Tell him just enough to spark his curiosity.
d. Assure him there was virtually *no* one before him.

6. Lovemaking affects *you* this way. It:
a. Clears up your skin, makes your eyes shine, and takes *years* off your age.
b. Leaves you feeling relaxed and confident.
c. Makes you feel like you just ran the mile in *under* four minutes.
d. Makes you feel a little sad.

7. You and your man have been to a party where he has flirted outrageously with an attractive woman. On the way home, he lets you know he is highly aroused and wants to make love to you. You would . . .
a. Make him wait rather a long time before finally being "seduced."
b. Refuse him, but in a charming way.
c. Be willing as ever.
d. Say yes, but tease him about the other woman.

8. In your bedroom, do you have a candle or some sort of special light to make love by?
a. Yes (you like romantic effects) _____
No (making love is fantastic under *any* light) _____
b. Do you ever swim in the nude?
Yes _____ No _____
c. Dance in the nude?
Yes _____ No _____
d. Go out without any underwear at all?
Yes _____ No _____

9. When you see a couple embracing passionately in public, you feel:
a. Envious.
b. A little shy—lovemaking is so beautiful it should be kept private.
c. Pleased to see something nice happening.
d. Amused.

10. You're feeling really rotten—premenstrual tension, unwashed hair, terrible day at the office—and your lover calls up wanting to see you. You . . .
a. Tell him you're not really in the mood but could you see him tomorrow?
b. Feel instantly better and hope the evening will end in lovemaking.
c. Say nothing, pull yourself together, and try to be your usual vivacious self.
d. Lie and say you have guests.

11. Your man is a marvelous lover except for one thing—he never kisses you on the neck (or caresses your knees or whatever it is you especially like). You would . . .
a. Subtly "instruct" him by kissing *him* on the neck a lot.
b. Tell him your wishes one night after lovemaking.
c. Tell him or show him *during* lovemaking.
d. Be happy about the *other* nice things he does.

12. He wants to make love *right* now. You're not so eager. You . . .

a. Tell him honestly how you feel . . . could he just slow down a bit and you'll probably be in the mood presently.

b. Distract him with drinks and conversation until you're feeling eager.

c. Consent, hoping to become more interested as things progress.

d. Lead him on, teasing and flirting, until you're both at a peak of excitement.

13. You sense your lover is losing interest. You . . .

a. Ask him why, and talk the situation out with him.

b. Reread the *Kamasutra* and *The Sensuous Woman*.

c. Start seeing other men and become slightly less available.

d. Do extra-nice things for him . . . small presents, *more* appreciation of his work.

14. How often, during lovemaking, have you done things that made you blush, or shudder a little bit?

a. Never. You and your lover only do things you can *both* feel comfortable about.

b. Never. You think anything you might do while lovemaking is perfectly *fine*.

c. Once in a great while when it was *really* naughty. (Not that you didn't enjoy it, of course!)

d. Often. "Naughty" sex is the very best kind!

15. Your man has been away for several weeks, and you're planning to celebrate his return. You would . . .

a. Invite his best friends to a dinner party at your house, then make beautiful love after they go home.

b. Cook his favorite dinner (for two), fill the house with candles and flowers, wear your sexiest dress.

c. Take him on-the-town—for dinner, a show—to whet his appetite for *you* later in the evening.

d. Prepare drinks and hors d'oeuvres, then leave the rest to nature.

16. You've had it with your man and want *out*. You . . .

a. Gradually stop seeing him, with a minimum of explanations.

b. Having been honest all during your affair, now tell him frankly you want to break up.

c. Find a new lover and tell him you've found someone else.

d. Subtly arrange for him to meet some fascinating girls.

17. During lovemaking, do you:

a. Remain quiet mostly, letting your body speak for you?

b. Whisper endearments in his ear?

c. Find that this is a wonderful time for cozy, *intimate* conversation?

d. Encourage or cajole him with obscenities or wild extravagant language?

18. You are at a posh party and your man asks you to go off with him into an empty bedroom and make love.

a. Since the project is apt to upset your hosts *and* your reputation, you gently refuse.

b. Finding the idea excitingly romantic and reckless, you accept.

c. You suggest, instead, leaving the party at once and going to your or his apartment.

d. You feel tempted and flattered but put him off until later.

19. Let's say you *did* go into that bedroom with him. Suddenly there are knocks at the door. You . . .
a. Say, "Go away, we'll be out in a few minutes."
b. Quickly pull yourself together, open the door, and say sweetly, "Sorry, we were just having a little private conversation."
c. Hold your breath and let *him* handle the situation.
d. Say nothing, take your time, and leave the room together, holding hands.

SCORING:

1.	a.0	b.5	c.10	d.2
2.	a.10	b.5	c.2	d.5
3.	a.2	b.2	c.2	d.10
4.	a.0	b.5	c.2	d.10
5.	a.2	b.0	c.10	d.5
6.	a.10	b.5	c.2	d.0
7.	a.2	b.0	c.10	d.5
8.	a. Yes 5	No 0		
	b. Yes 5	No 0		
	c. Yes 5	No 0		
	d. Yes 5	No 0		
9.	a.10	b.2	c.5	d.0
10.	a.5	b.10	c.2	d.0
11.	a.5	b.2	c.10	d.0
12.	a.0	b.2	c.5	d.10
13.	a.2	b.5	c.10	d.0
14.	a.0	b.5	c.5	d.10
15.	a.2	b.10	c.0	d.10
16.	a.0	b.2	c.5	d.2
17.	a.2	b.5	c.2	d.10
18.	a.0	b.10	c.5	d.2
19.	a.10	b.2	c.0	d.10

6-49: Lovemaking is not terribly important in your life. You find lots of other things to interest you, and probably the best kind of man for you would be someone who feels that sex is something one does occasionally but doesn't think about very much. You'll never drive a man wild with your sexual wiles, but then you don't really *want* to, do you?

50-119: You have the *potential* to become a wonderfully sensuous and accomplished lover, but, either through inexperience or inhibition, you are not able totally to let yourself go or express yourself through lovemaking. Perhaps you should read *The Sensuous Woman*, or better yet find a man who will inspire you to awaken in yourself (and in him!) the full joys of sensuality.

120-169: An ardent and imaginative lover, you have a healthy interest in sex that makes you enormously attractive to men. You know how to give a man great pleasure and how to incite him to new heights in pleasing *you*. You're a formidable competitor in the fields of love!

170-195: You tend to be *too* preoccupied with sex, which is both your strength and your weakness as a lover. Your overwhelming sensuality tends to attract one type of man, but many men are turned *off* by it because they feel they can't match your passion. Perhaps you have let sex become a substitute for achievement in other fields. You should try to balance your life by developing other skills and interests.

The Man In Your Life

You're a grown-up person *and* a liberated woman, but neither fact means you don't want and need a partner to make you *fully* happy in life. Of course, not just any man will do—you want a distinguished someone whose kindness, warmth, and strength are truly sustaining. The quizzes in this section will help you find and *keep* this paragon.

First, we measure the attributes of the current man in your life. Is he exploitative, irresponsible, a *user?* Or is your special someone blessed with a loving disposition and upright character? Can you afford *not* to know?

Next we look into the sort of man who is attracted to *you*. Men have their specific "types," you know, and it's fruitless to go after one who wants an Ice Maiden if you're Mother Earth. After that, we examine the balances of power in your relationship. Do you care more—and work harder to please—than he? Who is the principal decision-maker? *Which* of you is in control matters less than whether or not you're *comfortable* on your end of the see-saw.

Then, a most exhaustive quiz reveals if your marriage is in trouble—it's nearly as helpful as an expensive visit to a couples counselor. Truly!

Last, we explore that most fearful of bugaboos—could it be *you* (talented, pretty girl!) are a *threat* to men? Possibly it's *their* fault if you are.

Is He Fabulous, or Is He a Fink?

JUNIUS ADAMS

So you have a new man (or an old one you're still wondering about), and you want to know what to expect? Will he turn out to be a dependable dear or a repulsive rotter? . . . A jewel, or a jerk? Responding to the following fifty statements will help you find out. Read each carefully and mark it either *T* for "true" or *F* for "false," depending on whether it seems to apply to your man or his conduct. And don't try to guess the "right" or "wrong" responses—some failings are *virtues* in disguise. Just answer honestly, please.

1. He seems to like you a lot, but often for the wrong (to you) reasons. _____

2. He is sometimes a little mysterious about his past. _____

3. Though he tries to please you, that's not always easy. _____

4. He's proud of you, and likes to show you off. _____

5. He makes out an *imaginative* tax return and pads his expense account a bit. _____

6. He is fascinated by you, but doesn't talk too much about himself. _____

7. He sometimes seems grieved when you express an opinion with which he disagrees. _____

8. In bed, you usually do what *he* likes. _____

9. He confides so *many* details of his life that he comes close to boring you. _____

10. He sometimes talks about buying you gifts that never quite materialize. _____

11. He acts especially fond of you just after you've made love. _____

12. He's a difficult person to say no to. _____

13. He enjoys hearing about your triumphs and accomplishments. _____

14. At times he's said hello to people without introducing you. ____

15. He has his own private code of ethics, from which he cannot be budged. ____

16. Once or twice he's invited you to invest money in slightly confusing business schemes. ____

17. His temper can be a problem. ____

18. When mentioning previous lady-loves, he seems a little fond of them still. ____

19. He appears to trust you absolutely. ____

20. When you say no to him, he usually persuades you to change your mind. ____

21. He wants to know all about your sexual fantasies—no detail is too minute for him. ____

22. He's loyal to his men friends and gets annoyed if you criticize them. ____

23. He sometimes seems almost *too* sweet, for no reason you can understand. ____

24. He isn't always tactful. ____

25. Occasionally he'll ignore you when you're feeling loving or sexy. ____

26. He tends to give you things you need rather than gifts that really please you. ____

27. According to him, every woman he knows has some defect that makes her a less worthy love object than you. ____

28. He's not too good at making excuses or smoothing over misunderstandings. ____

29. Although you've heard him fibbing to other people, he swears he never tells even the *whitest* lie to you. ____

30. He encourages you to rely on him. ____

31. Your happy, cheerful moods are what turn him on the most. ____

32. Sometimes he surprises you by confessing to a problem, phobia, or infirmity you would never have suspected in him. ____

33. You can arouse him sexually almost anytime you wish. ____

34. He can't stay angry with you for long. ____

35. When he's late or fails to show up, his explanations are often a bit lame. ____

36. He's good at making love, but never says how much he loves you. ____

37. He can be terrifically persuasive and charming when he wants something. ____

38. He often conceals his problems from you. ____

39. His behavior can't be predicted—he often surprises you by being unexpectedly solemn, playful, or irreverent. ____

40. When he wants some special favor, he offers compelling reasons why you should grant it. ____

41. He sometimes forgets your special likes and dislikes. _____

42. He's been known to attack and disparage the people you like the most. _____

43. He's bored when you make shoptalk and will switch the conversation to a more personal track. _____

44. He's quite interested in your personal finances. _____

45. He has never accused you of lying to him. _____

46. He loves to hear about your friends' hobbies, interests, and faults. _____

47. Though generous, he neglects to make thoughtful offerings at special times—no flowers on your anniversary or bottle of wine when you've just been promoted. _____

48. He's kind and sensitive to your relatives even if he really doesn't like them. _____

49. He often makes plans *without* consulting you. _____

50. When he gives you something, he's upset if you don't make a big show of gratitude. _____

SCORING: On the following table, circle the numbers of the statements you marked "True."

1. G	14. F	27. F	40. F
2. F	15. G	28. G	41. G
3. G	16. F	29. F	42. F
4. G	17. F	30. F	43. F
5. F	18. G	31. G	44. F
6. F	19. G	32. F	45. G
7. G	20. F	33. G	46. F
8. F	21. F	34. G	47. G
9. G	22. G	35. F	48. G
10. F	23. F	36. G	49. G
11. G	24. G	37. F	50. F
12. F	25. F	38. G	
13. G	26. G	39. G	

Now count up the number of F's and G's you circled. The F statements are representative (though not infallibly) of the male personality we'll call the "Fink," and the G's of the "Good Guy." A "pure" personality of either type is, however, quite rare—most men have characteristics of both. To understand your man's rating, read the entire answer section rather than just the one that corresponds with his score.

Twice (or more) as many F's and G's: *The Fink.* This rogue tells you he loves you undyingly, but out of earshot speaks of "that sweet little deal I've got with a girl named _____" (And no matter how sweet it is, he's always looking around for something better.) He may be an ingenious and talented lover, but that's only part of a broader specialty, which is handling you smoothly, stringing you along, telling you what you want to hear. He only becomes angry or emotional when you won't accede to his wishes. Either he wants to meet your important friends and make them his own, or use you as a stepping stone to your *really* sexy friend Joanne. He also is likely to conjure up swindles in which you're to "chip in" on a house, car, camera, which actually end up belonging to *him*. He wants to know all about your likes, dislikes, and secret desires, because he plans to use them as push buttons to control you. This man will be terribly romantic and charming when he senses you're "off" him, then become cold when you turn affectionate. Probably he has romantic relationships you know nothing about. (Want to know where he disappears to for days on end? Ask your friend Joanne.)

Twice (or more) as many G's as F's: *The Good Guy.* Whatever his faults, he's a loyal person who feels committed to you. He likes you enormously, perhaps even in spite of himself, and intends to stay with you. Since he feels so committed, however, he tends to take you for granted: You're his woman, the courtship is over, and why make any further fuss about the matter? He regards you as an extension of himself and may get angry when he feels you're not behaving as *he* would. Though he's perhaps reluctant to put his emotions into words, his actions show he loves you. He dotes on your body, enjoys your personality, and sometimes can't seem to get enough of you. He likes to see you happy and productive and worries over your health and well being. He may not have much flair for tendering gifts with a flourish—having given you himself, what else is there? If he thinks you need a car, a coat, or a Mixmaster, he's apt to buy them for you, not as a gift but simply because they'll make your life easier. He won't, however, be certain to remember you on Valentine's Day.

Generous and dependable, yes. Tender and romantic, not necessarily.

Some girls actually *like* the treacherousness of the Fink (half the world's love songs were written about false-hearted lovers), and others relish the dependability of a Good Guy. Neither of those fellows, however, exactly suits most women's needs. The "fabulous" man is a mixture of both types. He comes in two versions.

More F's than G's: *The Charmer.* This man likes to flatter and amuse you, cheer you up when you're feeling down, turn you on when you're feeling "off." If he's sometimes insincere and makes promises he doesn't intend to keep, you don't really mind—he means well, even though he may not always mean what he says. In the movies, his part would be played by a Jack Nicholson, George Segal, or Warren Beatty.

Majority of G's: *The He-Man.* Though this gentleman may not be so adept at small talk, he's a *rock* underneath. He never plays games about serious matters. His method of courtship is to let you know he's available and perhaps to add, in commanding tones, "I want you." (If you feel receptive, better say yes right away, because there are others in line.) To cast him, you'd need a Robert Redford, Paul Newman, or Richard Gere.

HOW TO HANDLE THE TWO TYPES
Perhaps you're basically satisfied with your Fink or Charmer, Good Guy or He-Man, but you would like to *improve* him just a bit—get him to be more attentive or behave more charmingly sometimes. Here are some hints on how that may be accomplished—the tactics for each type are very different.

To get what you want from the *Fink* or the *Charmer,* you must assert yourself, argue, accuse, threaten—rather as if you were labor making demands of management at the bargaining table. Make a list of your requirements and insist on them. Tell him you won't sleep with him until he actually takes you on that trip he's been promising. Ask him where he was last Wednesday night and make him prove it. Lay down a set of rules for him to follow. Be ruthless, exacting, and determined (not grim, however—try to turn the process into a game. He *likes* games).

Once you've wrung an agreement from him, make sure he carries it out. Don't try to enlist his sympathy or appeal to his better nature. (Though he has one, it never emerges when explicitly called forth.)

With the *Good Guy* or *He-Man,* however, appeals to sympathy *are* effective while harsher attempts to impose discipline produce only hurt or anger. Really, he's not selfish but only trying to please you in his own—perhaps misguided—way. If you want something that he's so far been unable to give, take pains to make him aware of your need. This man's problem is that he views you as a part of himself rather than a separate individual. Desires you harbor that aren't the same as his just don't always seem quite "real" to him. If fresh flowers strike him as a silly waste of money, he'll find it hard to believe *you* want them, and never mind that you've told him again and again.

To get through to this man, behave in emotionally exaggerated ways. You are in *despair* over the lack of peonies in your life and *must* have them. When he returns with an armful, you show immense joy and delight. "How amazing!" he will say. "She really *does* like flowers!" From that point on, your vases will be kept full.

What Kind of Man Do You Appeal to?

MELANIE SULLIVAN, PH.D.

The man you're likely to turn on is looking for a special combination of traits you may not even be conscious of having . . . he knows his girl when he sees her, though, and this quiz is designed to help a woman discover which man (of all possible ones out there) has special affinities for *her*. Questions go beyond more obvious aspects of "sex appeal," as they must, since men pick women for the same intricate web of reasons that directs *your* choice of a sex or love partner. When none of the answers suits you exactly, pick whichever one is closest.

1. Your apartment could best be described as:

a. A cozily equipped nest . . . most definitely *home*.

b. A place you sleep in at night. Your life is enviably busy; why fuss with a *pied à terre* when you're hardly ever *in* it?

c. Decorated with a lush, seductive hand . . . all dramatic contrasts, provocative lighting, sensual textures.

d. Gracious. You enjoy elegance, want to share this pleasure with lovers and friends.

e. Cute. You like a place to look nifty, but can't see spending lots of money when imagination can serve instead.

f. Efficient. Yes, you enjoy pretty things, but you feel it's more important to create an environment that *works* for you.

2. You could be best described as:

a. Extremely outgoing and gregarious. Your phone is constantly ringing, and you have trouble declining invitations (even *boring* ones).

b. Quite selective about people you see; careful never to fritter away time with company that doesn't stimulate you.

c. An initiator of social gatherings. More than other friends, *you* are the one responsible for giving dinner parties, getting ballet tickets, arranging outings.

d. Stable in your social contacts. You rely on a small group of good friends, and are not really anxious to expand this close, loving circle.

e. Casual. You take people as they come (and go). Your social life is flexible, fluid.

3. Your bed partners are most struck by:

a. The tremendous imagination you bring to sex. You enjoy play-acting, using language that might shock *some* people, a smorgasbord of positions.

b. Your ability to share tenderness and affection.

c. A certain aesthetic sensuality. You feel the act of love should have as much precision and beauty as ballet.

d. Your frank insistence on your own gratification. You've little patience with a selfish or thoughtless sex partner.

e. Your sympathetic understanding of how a man's moods may affect his performance in bed.

4. Your style of dress is best described as:

a. Original. You appreciated the "costume" look when it was in and even now resist looking the way fashion declares you should.

b. Meticulously and beautifully coordinated. Wearing an outfit that doesn't work perfectly makes you so *unhappy*.

c. Erratic. Sometimes you look like Gina Lollobrigida, other times more like Marian the Librarian. Your style of dress reflects the mood of the moment.

d. Quietly stylish. You feel uncomfortable in bright colors or in styles that attract too much attention.

e. Attractive and dynamic. You've a small wardrobe of really *good* things that work together well, selected so you'll be able to dress nicely with minimum fuss.

5. You've a choice of these books for an evening's read. You'd probably choose:

a. *Falling in Place* by Ann Beattie

b. *The Third Wave* by Alvin Toffler

c. *Sophie's Choice* by William Styron

d. *Let's Get Well* by Adelle Davis

e. The *I Ching*

f. *Illusions* by Richard Bach

6. Which of the following describes your romantic history?

a. You are almost always the one to end relationships. When a man ceases to please, you're out *fast*.

b. Your attachments most often end amiably and by mutual accord. Once you choose a man, you stay with him a long time.

c. Sometimes you're the one to want out—sometimes him. In either case, you feel *torn* by the rift.

d. You are generally the girl to say it's over—but always accomplish this tenderly, with great care for the man's feelings and pride.

e. Most times you're the one to end an affair. But when he happens to want out first, you're puzzled and angry.

7. You've a selection of these movies to see. You choose:

a. *Luna*
b. *Bread and Chocolate*
c. *Bronco Billy*
d. *Urban Cowboy*
e. *Starting Over*
f. *Yanks*

8. Before you is a selection of gems all of equal value. You choose:

a. A ruby
b. An emerald
c. A diamond
d. A black opal
e. A sapphire

9. Your relationships with women could be best described as:
a. Often surprisingly intense and loving.
b. Rarely intimate; you much prefer men's close friendship.
c. Happy and easygoing, but usually not terribly close.
d. Taking place with girls whose professional and social lives are *less* dynamic than yours.
e. Gossipy and comfortable.
f. Happiest when friends are *younger* than you.

10. Assume you are a gifted singer. You'd perform in the style of:
a. The late Janis Joplin
b. Helen Reddy
c. The late Edith Piaf
d. Linda Ronstadt
e. Barbra Streisand

11. At parties you are typically:
a. Among the last to leave, after having boozily sung 'round the piano, and kissed at least three men you later wished you *hadn't*.
b. Rarely overtly flirtatious, but nearly always offered a ride home by an attractive man.
c. Involved in long, pleasant raps with two or three sympathetic strangers.
d. Listening to some unhappy man lengthily recount his troubles.
e. Talking quietly to people you already know.
f. Worrying that people aren't having fun, doing whatever you can to help out the hostess.

12. Imagine yourself a man. You'd most likely fall in love with:
a. Natassja Konski
b. Ali MacGraw
c. Liza Minnelli
d. Liv Ullman
e. Sophia Loren

13. In fantasy you are involved in a musical performance. Which scene appeals to you most?
a. Playing the harp with a symphony orchestra.
b. Improvising a jazz solo on the kazoo.
c. Playing the piano at home with your friends.
d. Executing an intricate sonata on the concert stage.
e. Conducting a choral group.
f. Strumming a guitar, alone or with a lover, in your bedroom.

14. You apply cosmetics:
a. Impulsively. Sometimes you make up with drama and dash, but you might rush to the office without even bothering with lipstick.
b. With science and precision. You've studied your face and use makeup skillfully, even when you're just jumping around to the dry cleaners.
c. Conservatively, but with *care*.
d. Very lightly, despite new fashions. For you, natural continues to be best.

15. Which of the following best describes your attitude toward psychotherapy:
a. You've never felt the slightest need for a therapist, rather deprecate those who rely on them.
b. Have found therapy helpful during times of crisis, but feel no need for it on a continuing basis.
c. Sometimes you believe most people (you, too!) require total psychic overhaul; other times you suspect therapy is a business packed with frauds who couldn't conceivably help *anyone*.
d. You're skeptical, believe people are more likely to be helped by loving friends.

e. Have never considered therapy yourself, but believe many other people are greatly helped by it, and think their needs should be respected.

f. Are in therapy now, feel no embarrassment about seeing a doctor who helps you feel happier, more active and more productive.

16. Which of the following men appeals to you most?

a. Marlon Brando **d.** Senator Bill Bradley
b. Mick Jagger **e.** Peter Fonda
c. Ralph Nader

17. Which of these best describes your attitude toward travel?

a. Nothing excites you more than the thrill of exotic places, mysterious tongues, unlikely customs. You'd go *anywhere* at the drop of a suitcase.

b. You enjoy travel, but prefer going places where the ambience is cool and easy. The noise in Tokyo would send you spinning, and you don't much like New York City either.

c. A marvelous once-a-year junket satisfies your yearnings for escape; mostly you're happy where home is.

d. You adore travel, but can't bear packaged or prearranged tours. You enjoy getting out and exploring a new place for *yourself*.

e. Frankly, you think the compulsion to travel is a little overdone. Paris is fine, but what pleasure could *anyone* find in some steamy Sicilian hamlet?

SCORING:

Step One: Consult the following chart to discover what kind of man-appeal you have. While we've identified six separate sorts of sex magnetism, you can expect your profile to overlap—i.e., you may be *basically* a (1), but with elements of (2) or (3). After consulting the chart, tabulate your answers, and go on to Scoring Step Two, which establishes the kind of *man* most likely to dig you. (Here, too, expect some overlap: just as you may share several sorts of appeal, so too will the range of men you attract stay flexible.)

	a	b	c	d	e	f
1.	2	1	1	3 or 5	4	6
2.	1	5	6	2 or 3	4	
3.	1	3	5	6	2	
4.	4	5	1	2 or 3	6	
5.	5	6	1	2	4	3
6.	5	4 or 3	1	2	6	
7.	1	5	4	2	3	6
8.	1	5	2 or 3	4	6	
9.	1	5	4	6	3	2
10.	1	2 or 3	5	4	6	
11.	1	5	4	2	3	6
12.	5	4	1	2 or 3	6	
13.	2	1	3	5	6	4
14.	1	5	2	4 or 3		
15.	5	6	1	4	2 or 3	6
16.	1	4	3 or 6	5	2	
17.	1	4	2 or 3	6	5	

Step Two: The number checked most indicates your primary type; the one checked next often reveals men you also attract, but not *quite* so strongly.

A preponderance of (1) answers defines you as a Child-Woman. You appeal most to the Fatherly Man who loves to indulge an impulsive, warm (but more than slightly neurotic) grown-up Lolita and finds you maddeningly appealing. This type is usually ten or so years older than you, and well established professionally, although he may be a younger man with unusual maturity and self-confidence for his age. Men with doubts about their masculinity are *not* for you; though initially attracted by your exuberance, they soon feel threatened and will *flee*. Actually, most men find your flamboyance appealing, but the ones who like to play Big Papa are *less* apt to be intimidated by your style than anybody else. Most likely, your man will be in business for himself (successfully!) or a high-ranking corporation executive or professional man. Psychiatrists especially find your complexities appealing.

Mostly (2) answers identify the Earth Mother. Because you've more compassion and tolerance than most other women, the Intellectual often finds you irresistible. This sort of man is generally self-conscious, nervous and easily hurt; you supply the balm his ego often requires. A second type, the Eternal Bachelor, when he finally decides to give in and marry, finds you his most probable choice; he yearns for a woman who can supply the soothing comforts of home without being overly demanding. Also, of all our women, you are the only one capable of "converting" the homosexual; he, too, trusts Mama more than most other females. Your most likely candidates will be found among college professors, poets, critics and journalists, musicians, painters and other artists.

A majority of (3) answers reveals the Loving Wife. Whether married or not, you are an amiable, affectionate companion few men can fault. Because of your genuine and broadly based liking for men, a wide range of types also attracts *you*. Since your ego is sound but able to subordinate itself, the Man of Genius is often drawn to you; this gifted one must be the center of his own universe, and you will make no effort to eclipse him. Find your genius in almost any field: the arts, science and technology, business or politics. Should you dislike having to cater to a mate with an oversized ego, however, you'll discover you also have a special appeal for the active, ambitious Success-Oriented Man. This chap will make a devoted husband as long as you accept one condition: his career comes first. Look for your success-hungry man in show biz, commerce and industry or professional athletics.

Mainly (4) answers indicate that, whatever your age, you are essentially a Free Spirit— You're open to life's adventures, as tolerant in your way as the Wife, but with none of her yearning for stable, rooted situations. Young, anti-establishment types are (as you might guess) nearly always eager to relate: you are the sister-lover they crave. However, you *also* have strong appeal for the over-forty businessman who, as he nears the male menopause, sees in *you* belated invitation to life, love and freedom. Your man may be a student, social worker, psychologist, small boutique or shop-owner or, if older, in business for himself or a corporation executive.

A lot of (5) answers designate the Cool Beauty: of all the women here described, you're the likeliest to subdue a Don Juan or captivate a millionaire. Because your reserve is never broached, your self-pride never dented, the Don Juan sees in you a ceaselessly intriguing conquest. Men of supreme importance or dominance (prototype: Ari O.) are also drawn to you. Only the impeccable *presence* you project can satisfy his yearning for perfection in a female. Aside from that, possessing you is one more way he tells the world he's *tops* on the status hierarchy. Your man may be found in virtually any profession, so long as he's *très* important, but have a special eye out for politicians.

Your (6) answers reveal you to be a Tigress, an active, alert woman who instinctively takes charge of situations (and sometimes men). You are one of few women who can successfully relate to sensitive, narcissistic, extremely handsome men. This type is apt to be talented but a little passive; you supply the energy and drive he lacks. Your passive-handsome man is likely to be an actor (even a movie star) or a photographer. Also attracted by you are men who *share* your dynamism; with such a one— likely to be found in law, politics or business —you could go on to be a world-beating *duo*.

Are You the Lover Or the Beloved?

IAIN STEWART

Adorer or adored? Slave or goddess? Do you live for him or would he die for you? Only in the most perfect relationships does the passion balance out (e.g., Romeo and Juliet; Elizabeth Taylor and Richard Burton, once upon a time; Queen Elizabeth II and her Duke). Usually a role is struck from the first, and sticks to the end. Your partner may be difficult, demanding, unfaithful, insensitive, self-obsessed, and callous, and you love *him;* or else he's all over you—your puppet—desperate, anxious, living for your smile, jealous, infatuated, and oh-so-thoughtful, just because he loves *you* with all his heart and time and money. To find out if you're a ragged Ophelia this time around, or an imperious Cleopatra, take this revealing quiz. And get *him* to do it, too, so you both know your place in the beautiful game of love.

1. When you meet each other, are you . . . ?
a. Usually late by accident
b. Usually late on purpose
c. Always late on principle
d. Reliably punctual
e. Slightly early, just in case
f. Invariably and anxiously early
g. Often somewhere else with someone else
h. Sometimes late, sometimes early, sometimes on time, sometimes not there

2. What would you most like to see improved in your partner?
a. His mind
b. His body
c. His bank balance
d. His heart
e. His problems
f. His bed performance
g. His social status
h. His manner
i. His character

3. If you don't get your own way, do you . . . ?
a. Leave
b. Lose your temper
c. Sulk
d. Shrug your shoulders
e. Get spiteful
f. Accept it as normal
g. Feel used
h. Reach for the Valium

4. What frustrates you most?
a. Being tied down to a single person
b. Being tied down to this particular person
c. Being involved in another person's life
d. Not being involved *enough* in his life
e. Not being attached enough to him
f. His not being attached to you

5. When you're with him, which word do you use the most?
a. You   b. Me   c. Us

6. In conversation, do you . . . ?
a. Ask the questions
b. Get asked the questions

7. Which of the following most closely expresses your main reason for being involved with your partner?
a. Love
b. In love
c. Want
d. Need
e. Affection
f. Money
g. Addiction
h. Convenience
i. Harmony
j. Company

8. Do you think your general behavior toward the other is, as a rule . . . ?
a. Too hard
b. Too soft
c. Too weak
d. Too inconsiderate
e. Too boring
f. Too out front
g. Too inhibited
h. Too fair

9. Which are you most often made to feel?
a. Guilt
b. Pity
c. Remorse
d. Contempt
e. Fear
f. Unhappiness
g. Insecurity

10. What tends to hurt you the most?
a. Being rejected
b. Being criticized
c. Not being appreciated
d. Being used
e. Being taken for granted
f. Being disliked
g. His toenails in bed

11. About what do you most like to be complimented?
a. Your looks
b. Your clothes
c. Your body
d. Your personality
e. Your efforts
f. Your intellect
g. Your style
h. Your character

12. What messes you up most?
a. Being what you don't want to be
b. Going where you don't want to go
c. Giving what you don't want to give
d. Hearing what you don't want to hear
e. Saying what you don't want to say
f. Living as you don't want to live

13. Which do you find is the most effective way of pleasing your partner?
a. Flattering him
b. Hugging him
c. Loving him
d. Making love to him
e. Taking him seriously
f. Forgiving him
g. Looking after him
h. Helping him
i. Teasing him

14. What do you repress most?
a. Your affection
b. Your love
c. Your frustration
d. Your sexuality
e. Your boredom
f. Your infatuation
g. Your guilt
h. Your true self

15. Do you tell your partner lies . . . ?
a. Out of habit
b. Because he does
c. To keep it together
d. To keep it cool
e. So as not to hurt him
f. For kicks
g. To maintain your individuality

16. In this relationship, how would you describe your ego?
a. A pillar
b. A rock
c. A diamond
d. A flower
e. A sponge
f. A grain of dust
g. A wall
h. A punching bag
i. A broken window
j. A weeping willow
k. An ever-open door
l. A sledge hammer
m. A butterfly
n. A river

17. When you think of the other, do you . . . ?
a. Glow
b. Melt
c. Wilt
d. Blaze
e. Shrivel
f. Glitter
g. Bubble
h. Dissolve

18. If you want him to do something for you, do you . . . ?
a. Ask him
b. Trick him
c. Beg him
d. Order him
e. Make a deal with him
f. Forget it
g. Persuade him
h. Cajole him
i. Bribe him

19. Would you say you tended to . . . ?
a. Caress
b. Pat
c. Knead
d. Stroke
e. Hug
f. Squeeze
g. Grab
h. Rub
i. Cling
j. Fondle

20. Do you like most to . . . ?
a. Give
b. Take
c. Surrender
d. Fight
e. Tease
f. Seduce
g. Instruct
h. Allow
i. Offer
j. Excel

21. Which do you prefer?
a. To take someone higher than he's ever been before
b. To be taken higher than you've ever been before

22. What's your most usual reason for making love?
a. Want
b. Need
c. Health
d. Habit
e. Generosity
f. Guilt
g. Duty
h. Hope

23. In bed together, do you feel . . . ?
a. Tense
b. Apprehensive
c. Relaxed
d. Hopeful
e. Fatalistic
f. Eager
g. Purposeful
h. Bored
i. Uncomfortable
j. Hot
k. Loving

24. What annoys you most about your relationship with your partner?
a. Its demands
b. Its insecurity
c. Its intensity
d. Its distance
e. Its hollowness
f. Its limitations
g. Its dishonesty
h. Its tedium

25. What do you think is your least attractive characteristic?
a. Temerity
b. Aggressiveness
c. Selfishness
d. Weakness
e. Viciousness
f. Cowardice
g. Lack of self-control
h. Dullness
i. Indecisiveness
j. Callousness

26. Of what are you most frightened?
a. Breaking up
b. Being alone
c. Stagnating
d. Being trapped
e. Being free
f. Going nuts
g. Facing the truth
h. Being left
i. Permanence

27. What do you most wish you were?
a. More disciplined
b. More gentle
c. More attractive
d. More demanding
e. More sexy
f. More difficult
g. More easygoing
h. More exciting
i. More loving
j. More selfish
k. More clever

28. If you could, which would you most want?
a. To get married
b. To have a child
c. To fall in love with someone
d. To live alone
e. To turn love into friendship
f. To turn friendship into love
g. To turn the tables
h. To start all over again
i. To be a different person

29. What do you most enjoy?
a. Being alone
b. Being together

30. What do you most resent?
a. Assumptions
b. Demands
c. Evasions
d. Lies
e. Blackmail

31. You like being with the other person best when he's . . .
a. Up
b. Down
c. Sick
d. Confident
e. High
f. Funny
g. Randy
h. Confused
i. Fast
j. Slow

32. Would you say you had . . . ?
a. Learned more from him than he has learned from you
b. Taught him everything he knows
c. Changed him a little
d. Changed yourself entirely because of him

33. What is most important to you?
a. Sex
b. Being in love
c. Being loved
d. Being independent
e. Your family
f. Your partner
g. Your career
h. Finding someone new

SCORING: Circle your answers in the chart below.

1.	a.4	b.2	c.4	d.4	e.3	f.1	g.7	h.6	
2.	a.5	b.4	c.7	d.2	e.1	f.5	g.7	h.2	i.3
3.	a.7	b.5	c.4	d.3	e.4	f.1	g.2	h.0	
4.	a.6	b.5	c.4	d.3	e.2	f.1			
5.	a.1	b.5	c.3						
6.	a.1	b.5							
7.	a.3	b.2	c.5	d.5	e.4	f.7	g.1	h.6	i.4
	j.6								
8.	a.5	b.2	c.2	d.4	e.1	f.4	g.3	h.2	
9.	a.5	b.7	c.4	d.7	e.1	f.2	g.3		

10. a.4 b.3 c.2 d.2 e.3 f.5 g.6
11. a.5 b.4 c.6 d.4 e.2 f.4 g.5 h.3
12. a.5 b.7 c.6 d.2 e.1 f.4
13. a.5 b.6 c.6 d.5 e.7 f.4 g.3 h.2 i.6
14. a.2 b.2 c.6 d.2 e.5 f.4 g.6 h.0
15. a.6 b.3 c.2 d.5 e.6 f.5 g.1
16. a.6 b.5 c.5 d.6 e.1 f.1 g.7 h.3 i.2
    j.2 k.3 1.6 m.5 n.6
17. a.4 b.3 c.2 d.6 e.1 f.5 g.4 h.2
18. a.5 b.5 c.2 d.7 e.4 f.1 g.3 h.4 i.3
19. a.5 b.7 c.5 d.4 e.2 f.3 g.6 h.5 i.1
    j.5
20. a.3 b.6 c.2 d.5 e.5 f.4 g.7 h.6 i.2
    j.6
21. a.3 b.6
22. a.5 b.6 c.7 d.5 e.2 f.3 g.1 h.5
23. a.2 b.1 c.4 d.4 e.5 f.4 g.3 h.6 i.7
    j.5 k.3
24. a.6 b.6 c.6 d.3 e.7 f.5 g.6 h.6
25. a.2 b.6 c.6 d.2 e.7 f.2 g.5 h.1 i.3
    j.5
26. a.3 b.2 c.5 d.6 e.1 f.1 g.2 h.2 i.5
27. a.5 b.6 c.3 d.2 e.3 f.2 g.5 h.3 i.6
    j.3 k.4
28. a.3 b.4 c.6 d.7 e.6 f.2 g.3 h.3 i.1
29. a.5 b.3
30. a.5 b.6 c.2 d.3 e.5
31. a.5 b.2 c.2 d.4 e.6 f.4 g.5 h.1 i.6
    j.2
32. a.2 b.6 c.4 d.1
33. a.5 b.5 c.3 d.6 e.6 f.2 g.7 h.6

WHAT YOU ARE

Less than 50: You have so little self-respect, its surprising you can carry on at all! The truth is, you simply don't *exist* without your present partner, and he probably thinks you're either mad or very stupid to be so thoroughly smitten. Actually, you give him every possible reason to treat you horribly! You can't possibly be happy with your lot, and life and love would definitely improve if you stopped behaving quite so pathetically and got off your knees! Until you do, love will be the death of you.

51 to 70: You were born to love rather than be loved, although the latter is what you most desire. For you, love is suffering, entailing few rewards and an enormous expenditure of effort. You are very sentimental, and think you know what romance is all about, but your passivity prevents you from ever giving firm direction to a relationship. Until you toughen up, you're going to go on getting hurt and used, since that's what you're really asking for. You need the pain to be reminded that you're in love, since you don't actually *do* much in a relationship apart from hoping against hope.

71 to 100: You tend to be the lover rather than the loved, weak rather than strong, compliant rather than demanding, the giver rather than the taker, but that's the way you are and there's probably not a lot you can do about it. Your kindness and consideration make you a good friend, but a somewhat unexciting lover. You put a lot of energy into relationships, though your efforts are only partially rewarded. If you were to assert yourself more often, you wouldn't get banged around so much!

101 to 130: You are balanced, normal, healthy, unneurotic, and probably happy. You make an easygoing partner and your relationships are sweet, calm, fun, and plentiful! Sometimes you are in love, sometimes the loved one, but either way you're quite satisfied. You are not a girl for grand passion and the tragedy that often goes with it, nor do you wish to become one. Since you prefer contentment to blazing ardor, you tend to connect with men who are balanced and normal and to settle into a comfortable future.

131 to 160: You are confident, sexy, positive, and successful at relationships, getting what you want and giving, often unconsciously, quite a lot in return. You're the kind of person men fall in love with quite easily, and this is fine by you, since that's the balance you like in a relationship. You are very good at love, and you've claimed just about the ideal territory from which to win the game without totally devastating your opponent. Your only problem may be with long-term relationships, since your inclination is toward quantity as well as quality.

161 to 200: People are always falling in love with you and treating you as if you were the most marvelous creature on earth, and you've got rather used to being spoiled. Still, you wouldn't mind being in love yourself for a change—all that constant adoration can be a trifle boring! You are not a particularly compliant person and can, indeed, be unusually selfish and unkind at times. Basically, you're out for whatever you can get. It would do you good to meet someone who pushed *you* away for once, since this would give you a chance to savor a little of that pain you have grown so used to doling out. In the meantime, you're generally surrounded by adoring men, so who cares?

Over 200: Love is not for you, since you could never hope to care for anyone as much as you do for yourself! Although you may have a retinue of servile adorers, they are more of a nuisance than a joy, and, in any case, most of them are slavish masochists! Basically, you want to be left alone, and if others were wise they'd allow you to indulge this preference. As selfish and self-obsessed as you are, you have little talent for relationships, and while men are easily infatuated with you, their devotion never lasts long. In the end, you are left quite alone . . . which is just the way you like it!

Who's Boss In Your Relationship?

LOUISE MORGAN

Naturally, people who love each other also have *power* over each other—but only rarely is the clout distributed equally. How do the balances weigh out in *your* relationship? Do you dominate your mate, forming opinions and decreeing friendships *for* him? Or are you a total yes-girl, never daring to contradict; molding yourself precisely to his specifications? The ideal is to *share* control, of course, but such blissful fifty-fifty unions are uncommon: in many alliances one partner calls most of the shots, while the other plays the sweetly *yielding* role. Now answer the questions below honestly, to see where you *truly* stand in the game of bosshood!

SECTION I

1. Check the tasks routinely performed by your man. (Skip those for which you are usually responsible, responsibility is shared or given over to some third party—a housekeeper, for example.)

1. Planning vacations
2. Taking out laundry
3. Balancing checkbooks
4. Preparing food
5. Budgeting money
6. Cleaning the apartment
7. Deciding whom and when to entertain
8. Shopping for groceries
9. Taking the car for a tune-up
10. Phoning to catch up on mutual friends
11. Deciding which invitations to decline or accept
12. Emptying the trash
13. Doing small apartment fix-ups
14. Jumping up to close the window when one of you is chilly
15. Deciding what to do on weekends

2. Answer the following questions with either "me" or "my mate." Skip those traits which apply equally to both of you. (Warning: though many of the characteristics listed are desirable, the "good" ones don't necessarily denote dominance—so tell the truth!)

1. Who is the more intelligent?
2. Better-educated?
3. More charming in company?
4. Better-looking?
5. More stylishly dressed?
6. Sweeter-tempered?
7. More independent?
8. More jealous?   9. More deceitful?
10. More ambitious?   11. More gregarious?
12. More admired by the opposite sex?
13. More affectionate?
14. More desirous of sex?
15. More beloved of friends?
16. More emotionally stable?
17. Who earns the higher salary?
18. Whose work confers greater status?
19. Who is more often home late from work?
20. Who is thought to have more "common sense"?

3. Which of the following adjectives do people generally ascribe to you? Which might better be applied to your mate? (Skip qualities which describe both—or neither—of you.)

1. Dashing
2. Brilliant
3. Reticent
4. Irascible
5. Intolerant
6. Cunning
7. Straightforward
8. Charismatic
9. Polite
10. Powerful
11. Good-natured
12. Tense
13. Determined
14. Hard-working
15. Flamboyant
16. Proud
17. Insecure
18. Energetic
19. Placid
20. Peevish

SECTION II   *Pick the most appropriate answer:*

1. When you're driving, he:
a. Assumes you know what you're doing and refrains from making backseat observations.
b. Directs most of your moves, never failing to point out even stop signs and red lights.
c. Kibbitzes now and then, sympathizing with your irritation over that tailgating station wagon, but otherwise leaving decisions to you.

2. You give a dinner party at which the guests include several of his most prestigious colleagues. Afterward:
a. He delivers a fair but not *un*critical review of your performance as hostess—your conversation was charming but the wine could have been chillier!
b. You both gossip animatedly, commenting on what was worn, eaten, drunk, and discussed.
c. You make a few suggestions about his career based on your new insights into his colleagues.

3. The two of you go bowling, and most of his balls go into the gutter, while *you* score a whopping 173. He's likely to say:
a. "Great game, sweetheart!"
b. "That pulled tendon in my wrist was really bothering me."
c. "I guess I'm going to have to work on my game."

4. He tells you he's tired of playing the leader in bed and wishes you would sometimes ravish *him*. You:
a. Accommodate him next session even though such role-reversal makes you feel a little odd.

b. Are pleased to do so—"taking" a man sexually has always been a favorite fantasy!

c. Say you can't oblige on *demand*, but promise to behave aggressively whenever you really *feel* that way.

5. Alas, you're more than half an hour late for a restaurant date with him. Rushing over in the cab, you:

a. Are reasonably serene since you *know* he'll forgive you.

b. Madly rehearse your excuses.

c. Resolve to be more organized in the future—and *tell* him so as soon as you arrive.

6. At a party he spends a suspiciously long time talking to a really stunning woman. You:

a. Insinuate yourself gracefully into their conversation.

b. Boldly interrupt their tête-à-tête.

c. Retire to the far side of the room where you drink a touch more champagne than you should.

7. He doesn't much care for your closest girlfriend. You:

a. Agree to see her alone most of the time.

b. Begin studying her to see if she really *has* the loathsome traits he attributes to her.

c. Expect him to put up with her for your sake!

8. At election time you favor opposing candidates. You:

a. Try to persuade him to switch over to *your* side.

b. Listen intelligently to his arguments to be sure you've made the right decision.

c. Aren't much bothered by this difference—silly to expect to agree on *everything*.

9. You feel both of you might benefit from couples counseling. He:

a. Flatly refuses to share problems with a "stranger."

b. Says that if that's what you want, he's willing to go along.

c. Asks what he's *done* to swing the relationship toward such a crisis.

10. You loathe spectator sports and he's a football nut. On Monday nights, you:

a. Read while he watches the game.

b. Compromise—he gets his football one week, your selection the next.

c. Encourage him to watch at a buddy's house so the apartment will be peacefully *bereft* of stadium noises!

11. When your mother calls to say she's coming to visit, he:

a. Insists she stay at a hotel.

b. Offers to move to the couch so Mom can share the bedroom with you.

c. Says she can stay at the apartment as long as the two of you needn't alter your *own* sleeping arrangements.

12. You'd like to quit your go-nowhere job and live on his money while devoting your energies to looking for another, better spot. He:

a. Agrees readily—career fulfillment is important to your happiness, and therefore, to *his*.

b. Tries to talk you out of the plan, pointing out that it's always easier to get a new job when you're already employed.

c. Aggressively opposes the idea—he doesn't believe the loss of income is justified merely by your hope that something better will come along.

13. He sleeps:
a. On the outside of the bed.
b. On the inside of the bed.
c. All *over* the bed.

14. You come home from the office with exciting news and find him napping. You:
a. Wake him immediately to tell him about your bonanza.
b. Rattle cups and walk noisily around until he wakens.
c. Let him doze—even good news can wait a bit!

15. You love chicken. He hates chicken. You cook it:
a. Never
b. Relatively often—but in a new way each time, hoping you'll hit upon a recipe he *likes*.
c. Every now and then, usually accompanied by a chef's salad or some other substantial dish, so he'll have something to nibble on, too.

16. You generally confide:
a. *All* your problems in your man—he's such a smart, supportive listener.
b. Only your major dilemmas—the petty stuff makes his eyes glaze over.
c. Very few of your own conflicts—*you're* the chief advice giver.

17. The type of happiness you find in this relationship is:
a. Quiet but steady.
b. Erratic—sometimes you're blissful, but you're often fretful and anxious as well.
c. Warm and lively.

18. Other men seem:
a. Not nearly as dynamic and exciting as your mate.
b. Sometimes very attractive indeed, but you're nonetheless *loyal*.
c. Often more glamorous than your partner, but not nearly as loving and sheerly *sexy* as he.

19. In bed he's:
a. Sensitive and accomplished.
b. Sometimes fiery, sometimes almost passive—he's a man of varied erotic moods.
c. Sensual *and* masterful.

SCORING

SECTION I
Question 1: Give yourself 5 points for every *odd*-numbered task for which your man is responsible, and 0 points for each *even*-numbered chore he generally performs.

Question 2: Give yourself 5 points each time you responded "my mate" to questions 1, 2, 3, 4, 5, 7, 9, 10, 11, 12, 15, 17, 19, or 20, and 5 points for every "me" answer to questions 6, 8, 13, 14, or 16. All other answers count as 0.

Question 3: "My mate" answers to items 1, 2, 4, 5, 6, 8, 10, 13, 15, 16, 18, and 20 are worth 5 points apiece, as are "me" responses to questions 3, 7, 9, 11, 12, 17. Give yourself 0 points for all other answers.

SECTION II
Give yourself points as follows:

1.	a.1	b.5	c.3	**11.**	a.5	b.1	c.3
2.	a.5	b.3	c.1	**12.**	a.1	b.3	c.5
3.	a.1	b.5	c.3	**13.**	a.3	b.1	c.5
4.	a.5	b.1	c.3	**14.**	a.1	b.3	c.5
5.	a.1	b.5	c.3	**15.**	a.5	b.1	c.3
6.	a.3	b.1	c.5	**16.**	a.1	b.3	c.5
7.	a.3	b.5	c.1	**17.**	a.1	b.5	c.3
8.	a.1	b.5	c.3	**18.**	a.5	b.3	c.1
9.	a.5	b.3	c.1	**19.**	a.1	b.3	c.5
10.	a.5	b.3	c.1				

Now, add up your score from both sections, and read on for a description of your situation.

320 to 240 points—*The man-dominated relationship. He's* the controlling force in this alliance, making the major executive decisions, and leaving you to look after more menial tasks. In nearly every intimate transaction, you accede to his whims, while he expects to be indulged and looked after. Very likely he's also top gun in the eyes of the world—though your mutual friends may adore both of you, it's his advice and good opinion they value. This type of match may sound unsatisfactory—and indeed you do have more moments of quavering self-doubt (and doubt about *his* love) than most women—but actually you enjoy some very real benefits. You're proud of having won so gifted a partner. And, admiring him whole-heartedly, you'd never even dream of straying —he commands *all* your attention, both in bed and out of it.

240 to 120—*Evenly balanced.* You two have different spheres of dominance. His career may afford more status than yours, for example, while you reign supreme in the *private* arena. In any case, neither of you clearly controls the union. Sometimes you're madly anxious to please, sometimes he's the submissive one, but each of you knows how it feels to be *both* servant and master, lover and beloved. Just one tiny problem: because neither of you is ultimately boss, you may find yourselves constantly renegotiating your roles and jockeying for position. Even as you're doing battle, though, remember that the presence of conflict between partners often means that they are truly equal.

Below 120—*You're in charge.* Most of the intimate decisions are in your hands, and publicly, too, you're the more charismatic, gifted and admired mate. Spatting is negligible, since he nearly always plays the appeaser, seeking to pacify and console you. Probably a part of you wishes he'd be more dynamic, but essentially you're happy with this easy-going companion, who frees you to aggressively pursue your primary goal—getting ahead in the world. Though you may have affairs every now and again with men who are dramatically different from him, you're never remotely tempted to leave him for one of those egotistical swaggerers. In fact, if you ever do change partners, you'll probably find *another* sweet, supportive lover to tend to you while *you* tend to business!

Is Your Marriage In Trouble?

JUNIUS ADAMS

Do you think your man is the dishiest creature ever to fill a suit? Are you delirious with joy at the perfection of your lives together? Well, my dear, get set for the But-I-Thought-Everything-Was-Peachy-Then-He-Left-Forever Blues! Or read on to find out just where you *really* stand . . .

Inventory of Marital Attitudes As far as possible, try to answer each question with your *emotions* rather than factually or objectively. (For instance, if you have thousands in the bank but nevertheless worry a lot about money, answer "not really" or "definitely not" to question 8, which asks if you feel financially secure.) You may check two or more answers to the same question, if you wish. You may also skip a question if none of the answers feels right.

1. Of the leisure hours available to you, how many do you and your husband spend together?
a. Most or almost all
b. A large proportion
c. Half
d. Less than half
e. Very few

2. Compared with the earlier stages of your marriage, are you spending more time together now, or less?
a. More
b. Less
c. Much more
d. Much less

3. During time spent together, do you tend to function as a unit, doing many things jointly, or to pursue mostly separate interests and activities?
a. Mostly shared activities
b. Mostly independent activities
c. Some of both, emphasis on sharing
d. Some of both, emphasis on independence

4. Does the way you usually spend time together seem . . . ?
a. Quite satisfying

b. Mildly satisfying
c. Somewhat dissatisfying
d. Extremely dissatisfying

5. Does your husband show enough affection for you?
a. Yes, definitely
b. Yes, more or less
c. Not quite
d. Definitely not
e. If anything, too much

6. Do you think he feels you display enough for him?
a. Definitely
b. More or less
c. Not quite
d. Definitely not
e. Too much

7. Looking back to the beginning of your marriage, would you feel affection between you has . . . ?
a. Grown
b. Lessened
c. Grown a great deal
d. Lessened a great deal
e. Remained unchanged

8. Do you feel you and your husband are financially secure?
a. Yes, definitely
b. Yes, more or less
c. Not really
d. Definitely not

9. Have you agreed on a general plan, budget, or set of priorities for spending the family money?
a. Yes, pretty much so
b. No, not really

10. You disagree about how money should be spent . . .
a. Often   **c.** Infrequently
b. Fairly often

11. Have your disagreements, lately, been ?
a. Less severe   **c.** Much less severe
b. More severe   **d.** Much more severe

12. On the whole, how do you feel about your husband's family—parents, brothers and sisters, other relatives?
a. Mostly like and approve of them
b. Like them, but with reservations
c. Feel mild dislike
d. Strong dislike

13. Now, what about his feelings for your family?
a. Likes   **c.** Mild dislike
b. Likes with reservations **d.** Strong dislike

14. How well do his family and yours get along? (If they have never or seldom met, make a guess.)
a. Very well
b. Fairly well
c. Uncomfortable together
d. Antagonistic

15. How many of your intimate thoughts and feelings do you confide to your husband?
a. Most   **c.** Some
b. Many   **d.** Very few

16. How often does he seem to confide his intimate thoughts and feelings to you?
a. Very often   **c.** On occasion
b. Fairly often   **d.** Rarely

17. Comparing today with previous times, are the two of you . . . ?
a. More intimate
b. More reserved
c. Much more intimate
d. Much more reserved
e. About the same as before

18. How do you feel about your husband's behavior in company—his manners, social graces, general way of presenting himself?
a. Approve, feel proud of him
b. Partly approve, partly disapprove
c. Mostly disapprove
d. Feel negative, ashamed of him

19. In general, do you think of sex with him as tending to be . . . ?
a. Marvelous, fulfilling
b. Uneven, some great moments, some bad
c. Pleasant but seldom thrilling.
d. Sometimes disappointing and frustrating
e. Quite frustrating

20. Lately, has sex with him become . . . ?
a. More fulfilling
b. Much more fulfilling
c. More disappointing
d. Much more disappointing

21. Every couple quarrels now and then. Would you describe your quarrels as . . . ?
a. Slight, not important
b. Sometimes serious
c. Often serious
d. Quite bitter

22. Do you have friends outside your marriage, whom you see on your own?
a. Yes, many
b. Several
c. One or two
d. Almost no one

23. Does he have outside friends?
a. Many
b. Several
c. One or two
d. Almost no one

24. Generally, how well do you feel you understand him, in the sense of knowing what pleases and displeases him, what his hopes and ambitions are, what he worries about most, etc?
a. Quite well
b. Fairly well
c. Not well
d. Hardly at all

25. How well do you feel he understands you?
a. Well
b. Fairly well
c. Not well
d. Hardly at all

SCORING: For each answer you checked, give yourself points as indicated. Write the plus points in the plus column and the minus points in the minus column.

						Plus	Minus
1.	a. +4	b. +2	c. +1	d. −1	e. −4	____	____
2.	a. +2	b. −2	c. +4	d. −4		____	____
3.	a. +2	b. −2	c. +1	d. −1		____	____
4.	a. +4	b. +2	c. −2	d. −4		____	____
5.	a. +4	b. +2	c. −1	d. −4	e. −2	____	____
6.	a. +4	b. +2	c. −1	d. −4	e. −2	____	____
7.	a. +2	b. −2	c. +4	d. −4	e. +2	____	____
8.	a. +4	b. +2	c. −2	d. −4		____	____
9.	a. +4	b. −2				____	____
10.	a. −4	b. 0	c. +4			____	____
11.	a. +2	b. −2	c. +4	d. −4		____	____

12. a. +4 b. +2 c. −2 d. −4   ____ ____
13. a. +4 b. +2 c. −2 d. −4   ____ ____
14. a. +4 b. +2 c. −2 d. −4   ____ ____
15. a. +4 b. +2 c. −2 d. −4   ____ ____
16. a. +4 b. +2 c. −2 d. −4   ____ ____
17. a. +2 b. −2 c. +4 d. −4 e. 0 ____ ____
18. a. +4 b. +2 c. −2 d. −4   ____ ____
19. a. +4 b. +2 c. −2 d. −2 e. −4 ____ ____
20. a. +2 b. +4 c. −2 d. −4   ____ ____
21. a. +4 b. +2 c. −2 d. −4   ____ ____
22. a. +4 b. +2 c. 0 d. −4   ____ ____
23. a. +4 b. +2 c. −2 d. −4   ____ ____
24. a. +4 b. +2 c. −2 d. −4   ____ ____
25. a. +4 b. +2 c. −2 d. −4   ____ ____

Of the two totals, plus or minus, subtract the smaller from the larger, to get either a positive score (more pluses than minuses), or a negative one (more minuses).

WHAT YOUR SCORE MEANS
Our questionnaire has inquired into feelings and attitudes that sociologists, psychologists, and marriage counselors consider important to good marital adjustment. If you were in a mood that is normal for you and answered the questions fully and honestly, the section of the chart corresponding to your score should rate your marriage as it might be rated by professionals. Since, however, some people tend either to be overemphatic or overrestrained in describing their emotions, our scoring cannot be exact for everyone.

You'll notice in general a positive score reflects positive feelings and a negative one negative feelings about the marriage, but there's one exception: A *very high* positive score is not a good sign. We'll start with that one and work downward.

Higher than +70: Assuming you're trying to answer truthfully, this type of score indicates you are compulsively overoptimistic and apt to delude yourself about the quality of your life. You refuse to see or acknowledge any flaws in your mate or your marriage and insist the union is ideal. You tell yourself first, then your mate, that you love him dearly and he's brought you great happiness. Sex relations in this kind of marriage are sometimes thought of as too coarse a thing to be talked about, but if not, you will tell your mate sex with him is *always* blissful for you.

You must realize you're pretending to be the person you think you ought to be, and to feel emotions you think you ought to have, doing such violence to your *true* emotions that they may bounce back in the form of a nervous or psychosomatic disorder. Some women, says Dr. Laura Singer, feel it's shameful not to have a happy marriage and will blind themselves to everything in the relationship that might contradict or disturb the illusion of happiness, leaving them open to shattering disillusionments when the truth finally becomes too clearly obvious for them to ignore.

Dr. Singer gives the following example: "A woman will come to me and say, 'I just found out my husband has been having an affair for the last two years.' Well, that's unwelcome news, of course, and she's terribly distraught, but where has she *been* for two years? She certainly wasn't paying much attention to her husband, or she'd have sensed long ago something was wrong."

If you're too far gone on overoptimism, you *may* not be able to kick the habit without professional help, but why not try? Start with little things: If your husband looks silly in his green Tyrolean hat, gently *tell* him he looks silly, don't insist he's handsomer than Cary Grant. When you discover no disaster ensues from acknowledging small defects, you may then be able to acknowledge larger ones. *Prognosis for this score:* possibility of violent upheavals or disappointments, and danger of marriage disintegrating into ritualized, affectionless "dead-end" relationship.

+50 to +70: Euphoric, "in-love" marital relationship. You tend to be too optimistic, but it's a sexy optimism, very good to have right now. You view your mate through a haze of romantic lust and uncritical devotion. Whether skilled or fumbling, his caresses thrill and comfort you. Your involvement with him is intense and may cause you to neglect friends and interests outside the marriage. Enjoy your euphoria while it lasts—it's as natural a state for human lovers as being in heat for cats. What's *not* natural, however, is for either state to last indefinitely, so don't try to hang on to your romantic feelings when they start to fade —the strain of trying may lead you to outbursts of anger or irritation, the classic "lovers' quarrel."

Actually, you should welcome periods when passion has deserted you, because you can use these times to try out a more realistic, down-to-earth attitude toward your mate. While it's not true that all couples eventually fall out of love, they do, inevitably, begin to spend less and less time being out-of-their-heads *in* love. For some marriages, this is a danger point. When romance dwindles, people who married because they were in love may find there's not much left to keep them together. They will then separate and find new partners with whom to play the love game, a common pattern with people who change mates frequently —Liz Taylor and Richard Burton, for instance. If you want your marriage to endure,

you'll have to learn to enjoy your mate's company under ordinary, uninspiring circumstances. *Prognosis for this score:* generally good, but difficulties in adjustment, possibly explosive quarrels on occasion. Crisis may occur if either partner changes to a less positive attitude toward the other.

+20 to +50: This score is nearly ideal, because it denotes both affection for, and a rather realistic appraisal of, your mate. Barriers to communication are few; you can explain yourself easily and feel few inhibitions about discussing your thoughts and desires. Being able to see your mate rather objectively, you can sense fairly accurately what his strengths and weaknesses are, and what he needs from you in order to function at his best.

Quite possibly, you love your husband and enjoy passionate sex with him. A person of your attitudes and temperament, however, is capable of finding satisfaction in a somewhat less involving relationship, with a man who is more a good friend and companion than a lover, for instance. Sexually, you're quite open and do not need the stimulation of extreme involvement.

If there's any potential source of danger to your relationship, it might be overconfidence. Just because you're handling your present situation easily and well, for instance, don't assume you can invite your husband's mother to come live with you, or adopt a couple of Ugandan orphans, without creating new stresses that could drastically alter both your marriage and your ability to cope with it. Another danger: Overconfidence in your husband might lead you to neglect him unwittingly. He may be a much more brittle, insecure person than you, and require more attention and reassurance. Don't assume he's happy or unworried just because *you* feel that way. *Prognosis for this score:* excellent. Trouble, if any, would come from a drastic change in circumstances, or a kind of benign neglect of the relationship.

+20 to −20: This score indicates a situation best described as *touchy*. Love sometimes turns to hatred through resentment, and though you try to be affectionate and considerate, many conflicts, rivalries, and thwarted expectations between you prevent the effort from succeeding for long. Ironically, this stormy sort of marriage often is quite engrossing to its participants, who can experience it as exciting drama with a plot full of unexpected new twists.

Both the couple and their friends may feel the marriage is romantic. Like Scott and Zelda Fitzgerald, couples of this type often play to their audience, exaggerating the intensity both of their disputes and their reconciliations in order to make a better show. For many years, even for the life of the participants, the touchy relationship may keep its delicate balance, but it is more apt to move in one of two directions: Either the man and woman become more tolerant and find ways to accommodate their often conflicting desires, or they turn more hostile. These people do not understand each other's motives or feelings with much clarity, often because they're unwilling to do so—to understand the other would be "giving in" to him or her. Yet the only way to improve the marriage *is* to yield, to start understanding and trying to cooperate. Why not be the first to try? *Prognosis for this score:* fair to good. The chief threat is that affection and good will may erode. The partners should be more conciliatory with each other, less stubborn.

−20 to −40: With this score, you should get immediate professional help. Your marriage has begun to deteriorate, and may soon slide too far down into mutual hostility to be redeemable. You and your mate have become antagonists—there are frequent angry arguments, or perhaps long periods in which you treat each other with cold disdain. You communicate grudgingly and have become quite uncompromising, insisting on your views and wishes and rebuffing your mate's. There is very little closeness left, just occasional flashes of affection or good will. Sex relations have become difficult or infrequent. Without outside help, there is little you can do on your own. Perhaps a good long vacation from each other might be useful. *Prognosis for this score:* If couple remains in same situation, poor. With counseling or therapy, fair to good.

−40 to −100: I doubt this was your score, or you wouldn't be reading this article. This is a dead-end relationship which, unfortunately, often exists between people who have been together for several years. They have retreated to fixed, angry positions and barely coexist, talking only in order to argue or berate each other. Meaningful communication is restricted to such bare necessities as "Pass the salt" or "I'm going to bed." Sometimes the couple will unite in making some relative or outside person the scapegoat on whom all the blame is shoveled, but being in agreement on hating a third party causes no spark of sympathy between them. Ironically, as in *Who's Afraid of Virginia Woolf?*, the couple becomes so engrossed in their hatred they have time only for each other and stop seeing friends or relatives. They'll never part of their own free will and remain stubbornly together until death intervenes. *Prognosis for this score:* very poor.

DANGER SIGNALS

Naturally, a loss of sex interest is a matter for concern in any marriage. It's significance in yours depends on the type of relationship you have.

- *Above +70:* Probably the sign indicates merely a worsening of the relationship rather than any pending collapse.
- *+50 to +70:* Very serious sign. A sex-drought will bring at least great emotional turmoil and, if continued, will probably injure or destroy your marriage.
- *+20 to +50:* Talk it over, find out what the problem is. Likely it's some easily relieved resentment or grievance. No threat.
- *+20 to -20:* Withholding sex is another form of quarreling. With you, though, not serious unless it continues too long.
- *-20 to -40:* Not good. Of the little you have left, much has been taken away. Further decline is indicated.
- *Below -40:* Does not apply, since there's seldom any sex in this relationship to begin with.

Here's how a sudden surge of sex might modify *your* prognosis:

- *Above +70:* Peculiar symptom for you, may presage a big change of almost any sort: a breakup, an improvement, even a nervous breakdown.
- *+50 to +70:* Not promising. Frantic emphasis on sex means you're hiding, afraid to communicate. What are you both afraid of saying, or finding out? Talk it over.
- *+20 to +50:* Iffy. Perhaps you've been too restrained lately and are busting out—*or* you're saying "good-by" to a marriage that's become unrewarding. Watch yourselves and see.
- *+20 to -20:* Probably nothing to worry about, just more of your shenanigans, *unless* your present passion was preceded by unusual, prolonged bitterness and ill will: That's bad . . .
- *-20 to -40:* For you, this sounds like the death throes of a marriage. It could, however, be an opportunity to get somewhere in therapy if you'll go *now,* while your psyches are open and in flux.

If you've just made a major change in *your* life, here's what it may mean:

- *Above +70:* If made with the aim of improving or smoothing out the marital routine, not much significance. Made in response to panic or alarm concerning one's spouse, the change *might* presage a breakup or a severe disruption in the marriage.
- *+50 to +70:* Has the change helped? Are you both pleased with it? Fine! If the reactions are mixed or dubious, watch out—explosion impending!
- *+20 to +50:* No threat. You probably had good reasons for the move.
- *+20 to -20:* Did you decide on the change and make it *together?* Good sign. If one of you acted alone, trouble!
- *-20 to -40:* Bad sign, whatever the situation.
- *Below -40: Any* change for these folks is good!

Are You a Threat to Men?

DAVID S. VISCOTT, M.D.

Do you ever have the feeling that you some-times turn men *off* . . . some subtle thing flows from you to them that they don't *like*—even though *you* feel you *adore* the male sex? This quiz is designed to help you discover how threatening (castrating) you appear to men. The following questions are meant to measure a wide variety of attitudes and ideas. Answer them as honestly as you can—give the response you really believe even if you aren't terribly pleased with yourself for feeling that way or know you probably should feel *differently.* Your *real* attitude is what's important, because that's what comes across to a man, and that's what you can change if necessary.

The test consists of a series of statements. Read each statement and mark it from 0 to 5, as indicated below. Do not mark any statement with a 5 (total agreement) or a 0 (total dis-agreement) unless you are certain you would almost *never* feel otherwise about the question. The questions are tricky, so think about them carefully.

    5 = agree totally
    4 = agree
    3 = agree slightly
    2 = disagree slightly
    1 = disagree
    0 = disagree totally

LIST A

1. If a girl can't tolerate her man's friends, she is not obligated to try to get along with them, even superficially. _____

2. If a husband wants to move to a distant city to further his career, his wife's concerns should come first. _____

3. If you feel your man needs a little prodding to ask for a promotion, you should push him even if he's not sure he wants it. _____

4. If a husband has annoying habits, his wife should try to change him. _____

5. A girl has the right to dress the way she wants even if it is extremely upsetting to her man. _____

6. It's the man's job to approach a girl for sex. _____

7. A girl should not allow a man to get his way all of the time even if she agrees with him. _____

8. Most henpecked husbands are inadequate. If their wives didn't nag them, they'd look for someone who would. _____

9. It is useful to remind a man of his past mistakes, especially when he's getting a swelled head. _____

10. When I want something I don't feel right till I get it. _____

11. A woman should never do anything she doesn't like just to please her man. _____

12. A man has no right to expect his woman to change because he is changing. _____

13. The husband who buys a new hunting outfit instead of a chair for the living room is very selfish. _____

14. If men get all the sex they want too easily, they won't appreciate it. _____

15. A woman who finds that her husband is cheating has every right to make him pay for it—and through the nose. _____

16. Old-fashioned or not, it probably is still a good idea for a wife to put away a little money on the side without her husband's knowledge. _____

17. When a woman marries she gives a man the best years of her life. Should that relationship end, it is only fitting and proper that he not only support her but also compensate her for the good years she has lost. _____

18. If you let your man get away with something too easily, it won't be long before he gets in the same trouble again. _____

19. You should never give in to your man in an argument when you are right and he is wrong. _____

20. It is only reasonable to expect your man to account to you for all his time. _____

LIST B

1. Sometimes withholding sex as a punishment is justified and reasonable. _____

2. It's a man's job to make good on his own without any help from his wife. _____

3. A girl should not lie to her man just to bolster his ego. _____

4. It is sometimes necessary to criticize a husband even if others are present. _____

5. Basically, men are overgrown boys and many of their demands need not be taken seriously. _____

6. A woman's work is never done, and having babies and taking care of a home entitle a woman to be pampered by her husband. _____

7. If a man is impotent with a woman, she need not take it as anything personal since it's mostly his fault. _____

8. Because men are less moody and subject to fewer emotional stresses than women, they should be extra tolerant of women. _____

9. If your man gives you a present you despise, you should tell him. _____

10. The girl who knows how to keep her man guessing and unsure of himself knows how to control him. ____

SCORING: Add up the numbers you marked in List A. Next, add the numbers you marked for List B and *double the total.* (That's because List B is only half as long as List A. If you got a total of 21 on List B, for instance, you should mark down 42.)

Add together your score on List A and your doubled score on List B.

This is your final score and you can look at the paragraph which applies to that score. *Before you do,* however, check back over your answers and see how many 0's (disagree totally) you marked down. If you marked *more than five* 0's, read the paragraph below.

More than five 0's: A large number of "disagree totally" answers suggests that you tend to be too submissive in your relationships with men, unsure of yourself, and do not assert your rights. Girls with over ten 0 responses are likely to be passive and unassuming to the point of being doormats. While it is true that they are not particularly threatening to their men, they are also not especially challenging, interesting, or exciting to them either. They appear undemanding and easy to please. Men see them as "safe." The irony is that such women are not usually submissive by *choice.* They fear that expressing their true feelings would offend their men, who could then reject them. So they keep their feelings to themselves. Thus, they may feel secretly resentful while trying to appear just the opposite. In time their resentment often leaks out with surprising results. They may then appear very angry and emasculating and try to control their men by being passive and making the men feel guilty. You just cannot be giving and understanding of your man if you do not have respect for your own rights.

A score of under 60: You can be castrating even if you are a doormat. You are *too* submissive. Your man cannot be sure you have any opinion, any wish, any desire, so he can never be sure he really pleases you. Women who swallow their pride, who play the totally submissive role, are not doing their men a favor; they even become like a weight around the man's neck. Everything becomes *his* responsibility and decision. When he is hurting he cannot count on you for support. He stands alone too much. Unsure of your rights, you need help in learning how to assert them. You have a right to be a person on your own, to find a job that pleases you, to have a circle of friends and interests that make you feel complete. You are not your man's shadow. If he thinks you should be, that's *his* problem. Remember, you have to be someone in your own right before you can give to others.

If your score is 60-85: Most men will be very much at ease with you, since you tend to be warm, supportive, outgoing, appreciative, and kind. You enjoy being a woman and probably have many men friends and confidants. In fact, you are likely to prefer men over women as close friends. You tend to be trusting and accepting and may give in to your affectionate feelings sometimes over your intellect: Frequently, you are the first one to offer to make up after a quarrel even when it's his fault. Flexible and not set in your ways, you tend to allow men to be what they are and to expect them to accept you the way they find you, and yet you are willing to adapt. You are not trapped into playing a stereotyped role of woman and are willing to allow your man to explore his own interests and to have a life of his own.

A score of 86-104: Although quite capable of giving warmth, understanding, and friendship, you are not totally open or trusting. You tend to make a man fight just a little for what he gets from you, and not only for sex. In the back of your mind you have a fear of being hurt which makes you hold back and sometimes test a man. When things are going well you can be a splendid companion, but you have high expectations which constantly get in your way. The fear of those expectations being thwarted often makes you defensive, tentative, and mistrusting. You can regain some of the spontaneity and joy that's missing in your life by learning to trust more and taking people more as you find them. As it is, men tend to be on guard with you and spend a lot of time trying to figure out where you're going and what you're feeling. You are exciting and challenging to men.

A score of 105-124: Men are apt to find you threatening! You tend to see yourself as a little princess and expect homage from men. When a man does not instinctively act in accordance with your wishes, you are hurt. You don't feel you should be expected to do very much *for* a man, however. Just being yourself is enough, you feel, take it or leave it! You may frequently give the impression of being sweet and kind, but men tend to be wary of you. You constantly measure how much you are getting and whether others come up to your standards. It's difficult for you to accept people the way they are because you tend to judge others by what you need and want. Men resent this, feeling they are not persons in their own right and are never quite good enough in your eyes. A man tends to feel you don't *appreciate* him and that you expect him to act a certain way all the time, whether or not he's up to it.

Your unreasonably high expectations are your ruin. Many women who are like this see themselves as God's *gift* to men. Any man who does not see them this way is rejected! Get off your pedestal and try to be a little more *human*.

A score of 125-144: You have real problems and are pushing men away because they do not pamper you or give into your wishes. If you have scored in this category, you probably haven't really grown up yet. If under eighteen, you can subtract 10 points from your score, but that's all. If you still score above 125, you are likely to be self-willed, self-contained, and unresponsive to the needs of men. I'll let you in on a great big secret. You are pretty unresponsive to your *own* needs. To be this closed to the feelings of others means you are also shutting off many of your own feelings. You probably often feel isolated, lonely, angry—and are unwilling to admit it. You wear a mask of self-assurance and strength when inside you are more the little girl who wants attention but tries to control people so much she pushes them away.

Men are likely to find you domineering, angry, punitive, and controlling. You want things to go *your* way and will take strong and sometimes unkind, action against your men when they do not comply. You are interested mostly in *your* needs, not in understanding how others feel. Your values are fake ones. You should stop treating people as things and start to feel.

A score above 144: There's a great deal wrong with the way you react to *people*, not just men. The great majority of men will not get involved with you unless there is something wrong with *them*, such as a need to be dominated and controlled. That means that the men you do attract are probably immature and looking for some kind of parental substitute.

Rigidity and control are the two big words in your vocabulary. You like to set the rules, your rules, and to react to your man when he breaks them as if he had desecrated a sacred place. Not forgiving or supportive, you create an atmosphere of tension in which a man feels as if he is constantly being tested, measured, and evaluated. It is as if the world you have built has no slack in it, no room for human error. In that way it is somewhat unreal, artificial, and stifling.

If you score in this range, you have problems which extend into all of your life's activities. Primarily concerned with yourself and with the effect of events on *you,* you need help to find a new viewpoint, a new sense of reality. You probably feel depressed much of the time and have a low self-esteem which prevents you from reaching out and enjoying other people.

Your Personality Index

These days, behavioral psychologists believe that how we *seem* to others is not quite as important as what we are "secretly" or "underneath." But some experts pooh-pooh this distinction altogether. In their eyes, we *are* what we seem. Since the personality we *project* governs other people's reactions to us, it's the only reality of *consequence*.

The quizzes in this section are designed to measure your impact on other people. First, your "social style," an incredibly important intangible, is assessed. Are you irresistibly charismatic or do you disappear right into the wallpaper? (Even a wallpaper girl can be perked *up!*) Next, we gauge the amount of approval you require. (If you need too *much* endorsement, take care—people will bully you!) Assertiveness is measured as well—and it's a quality that comes in many shapes and guises, some of which are *significantly* more engaging than others.

Do you let people *tread* on you? That's the question posed by another quiz, and if the answer is yes, you'll learn a little about pulling *out* from under everybody else's stiletto heels. Next you'll discover if you're bold or timid in your approach to life, generous in the way you treat others, or a niggardly miser. (There *are* ways to become *more* courageous and openhearted—we'll let you know about them, too!)

What Is Your Social Style?

CAROLE HAY

Does your whispery voice make people quiet down to listen? Or are you the one who arrests conversation with a flash of hauteur? Let's face it, our success in life largely depends upon how *socially effective* we are. A girl may be supremely talented, sexy, or capable, but these fine endowments won't help much if she isn't getting the right person to *notice*.

There are many ways of presenting oneself to the world, and each is effective in its own fashion. What's yours? Take our quiz and find out. (Once you discover your *particular social style* you'll be able to polish it to even greater attention-catching shine.) We offer no right or wrong answers, so reply honestly. To each of the questions below, check the response that conforms most closely to your own.

1. Your best friend has a new man, one you happen to think is all wrong for her. Furthermore, you have reason to suspect the fellow is a bit of a rotter. You would:
a. Tell her quite frankly what you think of the man and urge her to drop him.
b. Keep your opinion to yourself. She's entitled to make her own decisions.
c. Tell her that while *you* wouldn't have chosen the man, you respect her choice and will endeavor to be friends with him.
d. Be perfectly sweet and accepting, but let her see, by your lack of enthusiasm, that you have reservations about her new lover.

2. You've been to a party where one guest spilled red wine on your white silk skirt, another spent half the evening reliving his gall bladder operation for you . . . in short, you had a miserable time. Afterward, would you:
a. Forget your discomfort, write or phone your hostess as usual, and tell her what a good party it was.
b. Thank her, without commenting specifically on the party.
c. Tell her—what are friends for if they can't speak freely—the food was terrific and she was a fine hostess but you didn't have a good time.
d. Say nothing at all; you do have integrity.

3. Unexpectedly, you run into a friend while in a situation that's highly embarrassing to both of you—you're in a pawnshop trying to hock a camera, or you're both checking into a motel with people you shouldn't be with. You'd:

a. Ease the tension by joking about the meeting.

b. Say hello, without commenting on being where you are.

c. Avoid catching the friend's eye if possible; perhaps he or she would rather you didn't acknowledge their presence.

d. Greet him/her and give some plausible respectable reason why you're there.

4. A new job has opened up at work, one you could easily fill and would love to have. To get it, you would:

a. Go directly to the boss and tell him why you want and deserve the job.

b. Quietly sell yourself to the key people around him before approaching the head man.

c. Offer to do the job on a trial basis while they're interviewing others.

d. Let it be known you're available. Your talents and abilities are known to them by now, and if they want you they'll say so.

5. At a party, your man has been carrying on outrageously with another girl. You're feeling angry, jealous, and hurt. You would:

a. Leave the party abruptly.

b. Confront him and ask that he stop his flirtation.

c. Pretend nothing is wrong and save your anger for later, or possibly never mention it at all.

d. Try to break up the twosome by getting them into a three-way conversation.

6. A dear friend or lover periodically invites his mother to come and stay with him. Mother is stuffy, somewhat hostile, and definitely no fun to be with. While she is there you would:

a. Stay away from your friend as much as possible.

b. Continue to see him but pay little or no attention to his mother.

c. Visit, be charming to his mother, but leave earlier than usual.

d. Go out of your way to be nice—talk about her needlepoint, take her to the park, etc.

7. Two of your best friends have recently become enemies. You're having a party and would like them both to come. You'd:

a. Invite them, but tell each the other is also invited.

b. Invite them, making sure there are plenty of other guests for each to talk to. . . . Seat them well apart at the dinner table.

c. Graciously ask both to come but suggest they at least *pretend* to be friendly during the party.

d. Invite only one until they're feeling less antagonistic.

8. You're friendly with a man you've a terrific letch for, but he seems to look on *you* as a baby sister or protégé rather than as a possible lover. You would change his mind by:

a. Saying to him straight out, "When are we going to bed?"

b. Dressing sexily and giving him lots of subliminal "messages."

c. Telling him he attracts you, hoping he'll respond.

d. Relating tales of past lovers so he won't think you're unduly virginal.

9. A disruptive, overbearing person has started work at your office, and she's altered the rather pleasant atmosphere that existed before. She seems to have everyone cowed, including the bosses. What would you do?

a. Nothing, as long as she does her job well. You feel even *unpleasant* people are entitled to employment.

b. Stay out of her way if you can—dragon slaying is not your forte.

c. Face her, tell her how disruptive she is and suggest she change her ways.

d. Let the people in authority know what a problem she is, and suggest that the office would be better off without her.

10. You've been invited to cruise on a millionaire's yacht or weekend at a palatial estate—someplace considerably fancier than your usual social milieu. You'd prepare by:

a. Fleshing out your wardrobe with borrowed or newly bought clothes, boning up on the careers, special interests, and lives of the host and other guests.

b. No special preparations . . . it's *you* they asked, you they'll get.

c. Confiding to the host that this is a new experience for you, asking his advice on what to wear, how to behave.

d. Just packing your nicest things and trying to be at your best.

11. You've had to go away for a few days in order to have an abortion. You'd probably:

a. Tell many people why you went, and afterward give details of the operation.

b. Say you went away to settle a lawsuit or visit a sick aunt, and only tell *close* friends about the abortion.

c. Not volunteer any information, but tell anyone who *asked* that you went for an abortion.

d. Tell only a few people, and then make the trip sound like an amusing escapade (even though it may have been rather frightening).

12. It's late and your new neighbors are having an uproarious party that keeps you from sleeping. Your reaction would be to:

a. Call up and ask for a little more quiet.

b. Get dressed, knock on their door, and say, "You won't let me sleep, so how about letting me join the party?"

c. Wait until the next day, then tell them politely how noisy their party was, and ask them to be quieter in the future.

d. Put a pillow over your head and suffer through. Everyone's entitled to make a little noise. If they do it again, you'll complain.

13. Some friends take you to the symphony. Turns out you've met the conductor before, but he may not remember you. You would:

a. Take your friends backstage after the concert to meet the conductor. Once he sees you he'll probably remember and be delighted.

b. Send a note backstage at intermission, asking if he has time to say hello.

c. Tell your friends about meeting him but not offer to introduce them—you'd rather not risk a rebuff.

d. Probably not mention knowing him.

14. A male friend, in whom you have no romantic interest, starts telling you how awful his wife is. She's also your friend. Would you:

a. Encourage him to give you all the lurid details.

b. Stop him and say you don't want to hear anything against her.
c. Hear him out, noncommittally, without encouragement.
d. Argue that she's really not bad.

15. You feel someone has been intolerably rude to you. You would:
a. Stop speaking to him until he apologizes.
b. Tell him exactly what he did wrong and how angry you are.
c. Be polite but quite distant to him until he makes amends.
d. Change nothing in your manner—you don't want to give him the satisfaction of knowing you were hurt.

16. A good friend of yours is having a highly secretive affair. Although she's told you who the man is, she doesn't want anyone else to know. Suddenly, some people you know start talking about your friend and her lover. Your reaction would be to:
a. Stay close-mouthed until you can ask your friend if it's now all right to discuss the situation with others.
b. Call your friend and tell her that other people are gossiping.
c. Get angry. You've kept your bargain by remaining silent, and she hasn't policed her secrets as vigorously as you have.
d. Ask those people please not to repeat the story in future.

17. Your new man has been reluctant to include you in his life; you've scarcely ever seen the inside of his apartment or met any of his friends. When he asks you to hostess a party he's giving, you discover his facilities are inadequate—not enough dishes or glass- ware, mismatched silver, a dearth of pots and pans in the kitchen, etc. You would:
a. Plan to carry on with what he has—they're *his* friends and are probably used to his primitive housekeeping.
b. Insist that he go out and buy the lacking utensils.
c. Go back to your house to get the needed things.
d. This couldn't happen! You'd never agree to host a party for a man who didn't consider you the center of his world.

SCORING: Circle each answer you gave on the chart below.

1.	a.A	b.D	c.B	d.C
2.	a.C	b.B	c.A	d.D
3.	a.A	b.B	c.C	d.D
4.	a.A	b.C	c.D	d.B
5.	a.B	b.A	c.C	d.D
6.	a.A	b.B	c.C	d.D
7.	a.B	b.C	c.A	d.D
8.	a.A	b.C	c.B	d.D
9.	a.B	b.D	c.A	d.C
10.	a.C	b.B	c.A	d.D
11.	a.A	b.D	c.B	d.C
12.	a.B	b.A	c.C	d.D
13.	a.A	b.C	c.D	d.B
14.	a.A	b.B	c.C	d.D
15.	a.D	b.A	c.C	d.B
16.	a.A	b.D	c.B	d.C
17.	a.B	b.A	c.D	d.C

Now add up the number of As, Bs, Cs, and Ds you got. If one letter predominates in your answers, then read the social profile for that letter—it's the one style that describes you best. If two letters are checked with almost equal frequency, you have a more complex social type, and both profiles apply. *All* the letters checked evenly means you're a chameleonlike personality, able to present many different guises to the world. Perhaps you should become an actress!

"A" answers: Casual, brash, outspoken, you have great impact on any social situation you happen to be in. People adore you for the open, easy way you express friendship; they even like you when you're *mad,* because with you anger is an expression of how you're feeling rather than a put-down of whoever riled you. You've a great urge to *relate* to people and have simply hordes of admirers, from the news vendor on the corner to superstars other girls would be afraid to approach. Although you attract a wide variety of men, you tend to remain loyal to just *one:* Your passionate nature frowns on superficial fooling around. Often you're the first in your circle to start a new movement or rally people around a cause, but you're more of an instigator than a leader—patience, organization, and diplomacy are not strong qualities with you. Not *everyone* loves you: certain shy or reserved people find your aggressiveness a bit much, but don't worry. . . . Most people do feel better for having known you.

"B" answers: At first people may think you're stand-offish, but as they get to know you they discover your great integrity, good sense, and trustworthiness. You have a few really good friends around you, rather than crowds of accidental cronies, and with men you're open and direct. Love games are not your style—posing seductively *en déshabillé* or pretending to flirt with another in order to turn your man on would give you the *hives.* In fact, you have too much self-respect to play games of any kind—no hysteria or emotional fireworks, no name-dropping or chichi pretensions. You know your own worth and think other people should too—if they don't, that's their bad luck. This attitude gives you a strength people sense and respond to, though often without understanding why you have it. Though you seldom start out as a leader, you often end up in that role; you're someone who knows where she's going.

"C" answers: You could easily be a Washington hostess, or a diplomat in your own right. Cool, unruffled, suave, tactful, you can soothe the bitterest feuds, cope with the direst catastrophes. Fuss and fury are *not* for you, you believe in making the fewest waves possible. You're a keen student of the ways of the world and know that a few well-chosen words (though they might not be *absolutely* truthful) can often bring success out of potential failure. When you manipulate people and events (as you often do), you handle everything so smoothly that only the sharpest will realize they've been influenced. Sometimes you're accused of not caring, not being involved, but that's nonsense; you *do* care, it's just that you want results, not loud confrontations. Few who know you fathom what a full love life you lead. Love, you feel, is a private matter and should be conducted as a fine and well-orchestrated art, one that's as perfect as you are. No messy recriminations (or sheets) for you!

"D" answers: You're so modest you might be surprised to learn that when your friends start drawing up a guest list one of the first names they put down is *yours.* Faithful in friendship, loving and sensuous in a sex partnership, you're someone who's treasured by connoisseurs of rare and beautiful objects. In no way are you as defenseless as you sometimes seem. Your classically feminine "fragility" conceals many powerful wiles, some of which you're not fully aware of yourself. Absolutely *no* one gets so many doors opened for her or has so many of her vagrant wishes taken as absolute commands. True, you sometimes are intimidated by flashy people or get trampled on by hobnail-booted boors, but for every one of those, three or four treasures will come forward to protect and nurture you. Seldom aggressive in your own behalf, you can be surprisingly fierce in defending a friend or lover. Though you're not exactly a social leader, yours is the quiet voice that often prevails.

How Much Approval Do You Need?

LOUISE MORGAN

Do you live life to please your*self* or are you chiefly motivated by the need to win *other* people's approval? This quiz is devised to measure just that . . . to find out if you're the sort who'd do anything (or *nearly* anything) to win a scrap of praise, or if you're glacially indifferent to the idea others have of you. Remember, neither way of responding to people is *absolutely* good or bad; indeed, each mode has its own particular problems and rewards. So be honest . . . what you're seeking here is accurate insight into your own behavior.

SECTION 1: Circle the appropriate response to each of the following statements.

1. I do my best work for a boss who is generous with praise.

Always   Sometimes   Never

2. I would leave a job if not given what I believed to be an appropriate salary raise.

Always   Sometimes   Never

3. Speaking in front of a group is very difficult for me.

Always   Sometimes   Never

4. I primarily choose friends who reflect my own beliefs and values.

Always   Sometimes   Never

5. I automatically find myself flirting when introduced to a new man.

Always   Sometimes   Never

6. I am perceived by my colleagues and boss as a natural executive.

Always   Sometimes   Never

7. Criticism makes me angry.

Always   Sometimes   Never

8. I actively pursue friendships with people who appeal to me.
Always   Sometimes   Never

9. I enjoy being the center of attention at a party.
Always   Sometimes   Never

10. I am reluctant to share my problems or sorrows with other people.
Always   Sometimes   Never

11. When shopping, I like to bring along a friend whose taste I respect.
Always   Sometimes   Never

12. I enjoy spending evenings alone.
Always   Sometimes   Never

13. The company of strangers makes me nervous.
Always   Sometimes   Never

14. I'm a calm and capable hostess.
Always,   Sometimes,   Never

15. My favorite fantasy has to do with being famous and adored.
Always   Sometimes   Never

16. I refuse blind dates and unpromising party invitations.
Always   Sometimes   Never

17. When troubled, I reach for the telephone.
Always   Sometimes   Never

18. My convictions are deeply held and not easily subject to change.
Always   Sometimes   Never

19. Rejection in love immobilizes me.
Always   Sometimes   Never

20. Friends ask me for advice more often than I solicit theirs.
Always   Sometimes   Never

SECTION 2: Mark the following statements true or false.

1. I sometimes dream that I am suddenly unaccountably naked in a public place. _____

2. As a child, I feared one or both of my parents. _____

3. In school I was a high academic achiever but less successful socially. _____

4. My mother could aptly be described as a nervous, critical, somewhat anxious woman. _____

5. My moods swing from high to low and are usually unpredictable. _____

6. Relationships with men are more of a problem for me than any other area in life. _____

7. I have been in therapy or am presently considering it. _____

8. I feel envy when in the company of anybody more accomplished than I. _____

9. My sympathy for the underdog is easily aroused. _____

10. My childhood was troubled by poverty, family illness, or frequent moves from place to place. _____

11. **I was my parents' darling, either an only child or clearly preferred over my siblings.** ___

12. **I believe people who are always in trouble and asking for advice are** *weak* **and could do better than they do.** ___

13. **I have rarely regretted any of the important decisions of my life.** ___

14. **I am fully capable of taking care of myself, and if I had to live alone for the next ten years I could do so without serious unhappiness.** ___

15. **I earn more money than most other girls my age I know.** ___

16. **I established my independence from my parents early in life and consistently resisted any encroachments.** ___

17. **I have little trouble keeping a man's interest once I've decided I want** *him.* ___

SECTION 3: Choose the answer that most nearly describes your behavior in the following situations.

1. A good friend says she believes a lover is all wrong for you. You—
a. Say that when you require her opinion, you'll ask for it!
b. Beg her to tell you, in full detail, exactly what she *means.*
c. Let the remark pass with minimal comment —not everyone can be expected to approve of your beaus.

2. Boyfriends often remark that your behavior at parties is—
a. Overly ebullient and flirtatious . . . they wish you'd calm down a little.
b. Composed and gracious . . . you are *good* to be with in company.
c. A little aloof, particularly if you don't know many of the guests.

3. A man you've been dating rather seriously lets two weeks lapse without phoning. When he finally does call, you are—
a. Very cool. Never mind what his reasons are for not contacting you, you don't find such behavior acceptable.
b. Nervous and tremulous—you suspect you *did* something to prompt this defection or that he's simply grown tired of you.
c. Markedly cool, but you *are* open to explanations. Perhaps something happened in his life that made it difficult for him to phone.

4. You've just gotten a *sizable* **increase in salary. Your reaction is—**
a. Pleasure and self-congratulation. You know you deserved it!
b. A mix of anxiety and excitement. You love the raise but wonder if future performance will show you didn't really *merit* it.
c. A happy one, but you are also determined to step up your future productiveness.

5. You go to a store to exchange an expensive

purchase, and the salesgirl is not helpful. You—

a. Make a quick decision and hurry off.

b. Select as your ordinarily would without letting her attitude annoy you.

c. Take even *longer* than normal to make up your mind. Her indifference *irks* you!

6. You've written your first short story or painted your first watercolor, and you think what you've done is really *good*. However, when you show your opus to a good friend or lover, he or she laughs and says you're wasting your time. You—

a. See that the critic is probably right but can't help feeling hurt. Surely he or she could have found a *kinder* way of telling the truth.

b. Show your work to someone else; one person's opinion isn't decisive.

c. Disregard what the critic says and go back to work. You *know* you've got talent!

7. Your attitude toward subordinates at the office might be described as—

a. Consistently reserved . . . too much chumminess can corrode a boss-assistant relationship.

b. Amiable, but you don't have time to be best friends with *anybody* on the job. Too much work to be done!

c. Big-sisterly and relaxed. You don't have it *in* you to be a martinet.

8. You have a few too many drinks at a party and grow *very* merry. Next day, you—

a. Wonder to yourself if you went a touch *too* far, and vow not to mix champagne and bourbon ever again.

b. Laugh the incident away . . . after all, you were with good friends.

c. Call your hostess and ask if you did anything *truly* awful.

9. You've invited a good friend over for supper or to a movie, and she refuses, saying she just doesn't *feel* like going out. This is the third time in a row she's turned you down! You—

a. Grow indignant over what is evidently a snub.

b. Ask her if anything is wrong in her life.

c. Review your behavior to see if you've done some little thing that might have angered her.

10. Your romantic history is best described as—

a. Full of exciting, short-term alliances with men. Mere contentment tends to bore you and you quit the scene when coziness replaces passion.

b. Stable and focused on one or two quite important loves.

c. Generally stable, but you've had a more than modest share of flings and infatuations, too.

SCORING:

Section 1: Give yourself 2 points for each "sometimes" you chose. On odd-numbered questions, give yourself 5 points for each "always," 0 points for each "never." On even-numbered questions, give yourself 5 points for each "never," 0 points for each "always."

Section 2: On questions 1 through 10, give yourself 5 points every time you marked a statement "true" and 3 points for each "false." On questions 11 through 17, give yourself 0 points every time you marked a question "true" and 3 points for each "false" answer.

Section 3: Give yourself points as follows:

1.	a.0	b.5	c.3	**6.**	a.5	b.3	c.0
2.	a.5	b.3	c.0	**7.**	a.0	b.3	c.5
3.	a.0	b.5	c.3	**8.**	a.3	b.0	c.5
4.	a.0	b.5	c.3	**9.**	a.0	b.3	c.5
5.	a.5	b.3	c.0	**10.**	a.5	b.0	c.3

Now, total points from all sections, then refer to scoring key below.

Over 170 points: The Approval Monger. You lust after praise and admiration, and feel emotionally destroyed if it is withheld. Oddly, few people *know* what you suffer—on the contrary, you're probably the envy of your friends. That's because you're so adept at the art of pleasing (for you a genuine survival skill) and are likely to be charming, industrious, clever—the glittering center of everybody's attention. Just because you need admiration more than most girls, you're more adept at getting it. The price you pay for being the darling beloved: the lows that overtake you when adulation is withheld. Yes, probably you'd suffer less if you'd learn to find confirmation and self-worth from *within,* but be consoled: Your shining, amiable, so-seductive personality charms nearly everyone you meet.

100-170 points: Needy But Not Greedy. You enjoy praise and are exhilarated when bountiful admiration comes your way, but your sense of self isn't really dependent on what other people think of you. True, if nobody at *all* seemed approving, you'd question yourself a little, but you don't require endorsement from the entire *world*. This frees you to be healthily independent, even somewhat daring, and to risk other people's good opinion whenever an issue that truly matters to you is at stake. You can, for example, happily marry the man you love, and never mind if parents or friends don't applaud; or pursue a career that others think a little *kinky* but you find deeply satisfying. Your life may seem less glitteringly exciting than that of the "Approval Monger," but the satisfactions you enjoy are deeper and less ephemeral than hers. You've a right to be pleased with yourself—you need just enough approval to keep you emotionally in touch with other people, but not so much that you become their slave.

Under 100 points: The Free Spirit. You don't honestly care what *anybody* thinks of your life so long as it affords you happiness and gratification. You are innately daring and impressively independent, two traits that practically guarantee your rise to power and importance in the world. Because you so rarely yield to the consensus, you *can* head up the corporation, marry the millionaire, act in original and effective ways. On the negative side, though, you're not as sensitive to other people's needs and reactions as you might be, and can seem arrogant, even cold. Also, your relationships, though you're clearly on *top* of all of them, may lack sweetness and depth. Dauntless you are, and a natural leader . . . just take care not to allow your intrepid spirit to cut you *off* from other less monumentally self-reliant people.

Are You an Assertive Girl?

CAROLE HAY

Are you a strong, forthright person who easily makes her wishes known and will fight to see them realized? Or a self-effacing girl who yearns to assert herself with greater *force*? You may actually be more powerful than you think—or *less!* So why not take our test and find out how you rate? After each question, check the answer which seems closest to how *you* would react in the situation described.

1. Your doctor is being a little dense—although you've described a set of symptoms twice (you're anxious, irritable, and can't sleep), he persists in asking unrelated questions about your *periods*. You would:
a. Think he probably believes your problems are *tied in* with menstruation, and continue to answer him.
b. Decide not to prolong a fruitless dialogue, say "thank you" and depart—with no intention of coming *back*.
c. Say, "I think you misunderstood," and explain your symptoms again, this time in more detail.
d. Ask the doctor *why* he thinks you have a menstrual problem when you were complaining about something else entirely.

2. In a dress shop, a trying-to-be-helpful saleslady keeps suggesting you accept *her* selections. Having finally narrowed your search down to two choices, you would:
a. Say, "I really need to come to my *own* decision about these."

b. Quietly tune her out while you decide.
c. Tend to give her opinion some consideration—after all, she does know which styles are newest.
d. Feel vindicated when you choose the dress she does *not* favor.

3. You're being interviewed for a job when suddenly the interviewer says you don't seem to have enough background for the position. You'd probably respond:
a. "Perhaps you're right, but I learn quickly and think I could handle the work."
b. "I guess I don't agree with you. I really *am* well qualified." Then describe the responsibilities of your last job.

c. By asking what background she's looking for and then trying to show ways in which your previous job *did* require many of the same skills.

d. By enumerating the duties you feel the job would require and explaining how you'd perform each of them.

4. Sex with your new lover is wonderful, except that he likes one particular "variation" which turns you off! You'd:

a. Refuse to go along—sexual acts can't be fun unless *mutually* enjoyable.

b. Explain why you'd rather not, for now at least . . . maybe sometime soon you'll change your mind.

c. Indulge him occasionally.

d. Try to make him happy—you're sure he'd do the same for you!

5. The office chauvinist can't resist making sexist observations at every office conference. When he says, "Turning, now, to the 'woman's page,' we'll listen to Cindy present *her* statistics," you would:

a. Simply ignore him . . . he's just making himself look silly.

b. Say, "Bernie, I love you, but *must* you keep making those silly cracks?"

c. Tell him later that his remarks upset you and to please stop making them.

d. Get back at him by subtly lighting into one of *his* reports.

6. A good friend of yours has one bad trait. She continually borrows small sums of money and never repays. You'd:

a. Ask for the money back every time until repayment becomes automatic.

b. Ignore it. If she has some quirky reason for wanting to keep the money, let her.

c. Remind her from time to time that she owes you money, but without demanding she return it.

d. Next time she asks, say, "If you want me to *give* you money, Marie, I will, but if this is a loan I'd like it back."

7. A couple you know gives frequent dinner parties where the meal seldom arrives before eleven or midnight. When invited to their house you would:

a. Accept, then inquire jokingly, "Until what hour will you starve us?"

b. Accept, but say you grow *faint* unless you eat by eight!

c. Snack before you go.

d. Go, since they promise to serve dinner at a reasonable hour. When the time comes, ask how soon the meal will be.

8. On vacation, you arrive at your hotel with a confirmed reservation only to find they haven't any room and are sending you to another, less desirable hotel. You:

a. Depart angrily, letting them know you're going to complain to the tourist bureau.

b. Call for the manager and tell him how much you had *counted* on staying at his hotel.

c. Say you don't accept that solution and keep bugging the desk clerk until he *finds* you a suitable room.

d. Ask for the manager, demand to know whether any rooms are vacant. If so, insist you are entitled to one.

9. You've been looking forward to a lovely birthday celebration or a present from your man but he forgets the occasion. You'd probably:

a. Say, "I'm hurt—you didn't remember today's my birthday."

b. See no reason to make *him* feel bad—forgive his forgetfulness.

c. Say, "This is a rather *special* day," and hope he does something, even at the last minute.

d. Scold him—you'd never forget *his* birthday.

10. For years a dear aunt has celebrated Easter Sunday by taking you out to brunch at a fancy-but-stodgy restaurant. As a child you found these occasions thrilling, but lately they've bored your considerably. You:

a. Continue the luncheons anyway. They're a tradition now, and mean a lot to your aunt.

b. Suggest the outings have become too expensive. Perhaps you could just drop by her house, instead.

c. Tell her you love her very much, but you're grown up now and like to go out of town over the long holiday.

d. Insist it's your turn to treat and then take her to *your* favorite restaurant.

11. Your company's new vice president credits the office routing-system *you* devised to George. You:

a. Think little of it . . . other, more important execs *know* you're responsible for the change.

b. Wait for George to speak . . . it's up to *him* to rectify the error.

c. Amend the mistake quietly but firmly. "Excuse me, but *I* was the one who drew up the system."

d. Correct the boss good-humoredly: "Listen, George is great, but don't deprive me of my moment of glory! That system was *my* idea!"

12. The same absent-minded V.P. credits you with one of *George's* ideas. You would:

a. Say nothing—let George speak up if he wants to.

b. Feel embarrassed at being wrongly praised, but not enough to contradict the boss.

c. Smile and wink conspiratorily at George.

d. Tell the boss that George deserves credit for the idea.

13. A friend has become so critical of you she could pass for an enemy. She is appalled by your $40 haircut, suspects your boyfriend has homosexual tendencies, and wonders why you always pick such losers. You:

a. Resent her but listen anyway—even the most unreasonable criticism usually has *some* basis in fact.

b. Ask what's been making her so bitchy lately. *Why* is she angry at you?

c. Tell her she must either let up or you'll end the relationship. You don't *need* to be put down by friends.

d. Feel annoyed and arrange to see less of her in the future.

14. Your love life has been almost totally arid for the past year. When a devastatingly attractive man starts working at your office, you:

a. Manage to find several excuses a day to go in to see him.

b. Arrange to have lunch on some pretext, and, once he's across the table from you, flirt adroitly.

c. Invite him to your place for dinner . . . why not be *direct*?

d. Be especially bright, sweet, and attentive around him. He'll soon notice how attractive you are.

SCORING: Circle your answers in the chart below.

1.	a.Z	b.Y	c.X	d.W
2.	a.X	b.Y	c.Z	d.W

3.	a.Z	b.Y	c.X	d.W
4.	a.W	b.X	c.Y	d.Z
5.	a.Z	b.Y	c.X	d.W
6.	a.W	b.Z	c.Y	d.X
7.	a.Y	b.W	c.Z	d.X
8.	a.Z	b.Y	c.W	d.X
9.	a.X	b.Z	c.Y	d.W
10.	a.Z	b.Y	c.W	d.X
11.	a.Z	b.Y	c.W	d.X
12.	a.W	b.Z	c.Y	d.X
13.	a.Z	b.X	c.W	d.Y
14.	a.Y	b.X	c.W	d.Z

Count up the number of W, X, Y, and Z choices, then read the description of your predominant letter to find out your degree of assertiveness. Don't expect a totally consistent score, though . . . most people are underassertive in *some* situations, *over*assertive in others. These extreme choices show the kind of situations that make you particularly anxious, guilt-ridden, or defensive. After you've determined your *general* style, you can work on problem areas!

W: Boss Lady You'll never need anyone to help look out for *your* interests. Confident of who you are and what you want, you almost *dare* the world to stop you from achieving goals. Though quite capable of fighting to win an objective, you rarely need to—people sense that fierce determination and give way before it. As powerfully effective as you are, though, you sometimes react more *defensively* than you must, thereby closing other people out. Indeed, your ego and will are so potent that would-be friends and lovers are sometimes *afraid* to approach you. You're already quite impressive, but you'd be *happier* if you could relax a bit more and become more accepting of possible "slights."

X: The Politician You are the confident, outgoing girl who's able to express your desires easily and pursue them without inhibitions. Better yet, you lack the occasional ferocity of the superassertive girl, and rarely push your will forward unless it's truly warranted. Though healthily assertive, you're also deeply *rational* and are likely to come up with smart compromise solutions when confronted by a dilemma. Why jeopardize fine relationships by bending people to your will when you can more easily "settle"? Congratulations, your truly *generous* form of assertiveness is the best of all.

Y: Disciplined Achiever You are, above all, smoothly graceful in all your social dealings—in a word, *civilized*. You loathe extremes and prefer to communicate your needs and desires in a subdued, understated way. You'll tell someone if you're angry or pleased, but so quietly that unless the person is supersensitive he'll never know how *intensely* you feel. Yes, your cool is much admired, but being a bit less rigorously controlled *could* make life more exciting.

Z: Sweet Sympathizer Kind and considerate, you thrive in gentle and understanding company. Aggressive, egotistical folk are a *problem*, however. When people are rude or pushy, you never quite find the words to rebuke them and allow yourself to be overruled or embarrassed rather than cause a dispute. You may fight back with surprising spirit, but ordinarily you will sacrifice your own interests in order to maintain harmony. True, you're wonderfully easy to get along with, but wouldn't you like to have things go *your* way a little more often? Then you'd better start speaking *up*.

How Much Guff Do You Take?

CAROLE HAY

Are you an adorably accommodating door-mat? . . . a sensible person who knows how and when to stand up for her rights? . . . Or a spitfire, taking no guff from *anybody?* Answer the questions below as truthfully as you can and find out how *you* handle the blows the world hands you. For each situation, pick the reaction *closest* to what yours would probably be. Don't try to be too consistent: the answers may seem obvious, but the scoring is tricky and *allows* for an occasional answer that is out-of-character—overly tame or overly tough.

1. A boor is brought to a party you are giving. He eats everything in sight, dominates the conversation, and insults you and your friends. You would:

a. Tend to be charitable, understanding that the poor man is driven by a massive inferiority complex.

b. Be quite firm and ask him to leave the party . . . don't back down even if he's difficult.

c. Attempt to distract him by sitting him down with a book on some subject you know interests him.

d. Appeal to whoever brought him ("Will you please try to control your friend—or maybe take him *home?*").

e. Explain to each guest (or call them the next day) that this man isn't your friend . . . and you're terribly sorry.

2. Your lover's ex-wife calls and demands money beyond what the court has allotted her. You haven't had a meal out, thrown a good party or had any perfume for *weeks*. He gives her $200. Next week you hear she has given a luau featuring roast suckling pig. You react by:

a. Thinking seriously of breaking off with him.

b. Mentioning the things you'd like to have until he sees what's wrong.

c. Getting *very* angry . . . you have it out over a lengthy chat.

d. Understanding that he still feels a strong obligation toward her, even though you know he'll eventually be yours alone.

e. Telling him he must be more generous with *you.*

3. Tired of your usual self-destructing pantyhose, you go to the most expensive store in town to buy really good ones. The saleslady is snooty and obviously thinks your $48 dress doesn't compare with her regular customers' $500 numbers. However, twenty minutes after you put on the pantyhose, they run. You:

a. Go back, authoritatively confront the saleslady, and *insist* on having your money refunded.

b. Decide to forget about the incident, and dash out to buy another pair at the supermarket.

c. Make the store replace the pantyhose without anger or scene-making.

d. Write a strongly worded complaint to the store, mentioning the saleslady who waited on you.

e. Tell your friends and relatives not to buy from that store.

4. In your adult life, have you ever been driven to physical violence—slapped someone, pummeled, attacked with pointy fingernails?

a. "It's happened."

b. No. Even though you might have wanted to, civilized people just don't *hit* each other.

c. Fairly often—with *men* you think a certain amount of violence is sexually exciting.

d. Never. You're a peaceful person without violent impulses.

e. No, but sometimes you daydream of really letting somebody *have* it.

5. At a dinner party, a supercilious lady seems bent on proving her superiority. You say you summer in Fire Island. *She* says Fire Island is sleazy compared to Cap d'Antibes. You compliment the soufflé. *She* says it's almost as good as the one she was served by Princess Grace. You:

a. Become silent—you have no desire to compete with this jet-setty hotshot.

b. Find her interesting—where *else* could you hear firsthand accounts of Grace's dinner table?

c. Are sweet and wide-eyed, lead her on to more tales of her fantastic life until everybody else at the table hates her, too.

d. Tell her that *you* hope to be as experienced as she when you're her *age.*

e. Fight back with names and places of your *own.*

6. This is the *second* time some man at your office has been promoted while you, with much more experience and knowhow, are still in an assistant's job. You would:

a. Say nothing, but start looking for another position. When they see that some other company is happy to make you an executive, your employers will learn a lesson.

b. Go speak to your boss and politely tell him he's making a mistake: not only is sexual discrimination illegal, but you would have done *better* than either of the two men who were promoted.

c. Sweetly announce that unless you get the *next* promotion you're leaving.

d. Organize a Women's Lib movement in the company to fight for *all* the female employees' rights.

7. His mother cannot understand or *stand* your living together. She is critical of everything: your decorating, friends, pets, business life, children (or lack thereof), even your Billy Joel records. You:

a. Treat her so sweetly she can't *help* but approve—albeit reluctantly.

b. *Hide* the raunchier parts of your life from her and keep your more eccentric friends out of her path.

c. See her only when unavoidable.

d. Discuss the problem with her and try to convince her your life is right for *you.*

e. *Overwhelm* her with modernity, chic, superiority until she *knows* you're terrific even if she won't admit it.

8. An annoying neighbor plays Fats Waller records until 5:00 A.M., borrows sugar, petty cash, coffee, onions, etc., and asks you to "sit" his miniature poodle. You:

a. Joke about him to your friends—he makes a *very* funny story!

b. Eventually get furious, march to his door and tell him off.

c. Hint about how you like to get to sleep early, need your onions for your own *boeuf bourguignon.*

d. Defend yourself with handy little *lies:* you're out of sugar, cash, and your pussycat is *vicious* with dogs. . . .

e. Make *practical* suggestions: "If you moved your hi-fi away from the wall, perhaps I could sleep."

9. You've been going with a married man for some time. He's promised love eternal and marriage eventual. Then you find out he's been lying: his wife believes him happily in love with her, and he's never even *broached* divorce. You would:

a. Walk away, disillusioned, without a backward glance.

b. Call his wife and have a "little talk."

c. Suffer for a while, then decide never to trust a married man ever again and *stick* to it!

d. Consult with your best friend(s) on ploys to get him away from his wife for *good.*

10. It's raining *floods* and you've been trying to hail a cab for the last twenty minutes. Finally, an empty taxi pulls up, but as you're about to step inside, a feisty old lady you hadn't noticed before pushes in front of you and says, "I was here first." You:

a. Ask her which way she wants to go and suggest you share the cab.

b. Are mad enough to kill but let her have it. . . . Maybe she was there first and, besides, it's no *fun* to fight with little old ladies.

c. Invent some reason you *must* have the taxi —your pains are coming every three minutes now, or, you're late for an important job interview—and hope she'll be sympathetic.

d. Say, "Sorry, you're mistaken. I was waiting here long before you arrived," nudge her gently aside and get *in.*

11. A friend or fellow-worker is always stealing your ideas and passing them off as her own. You discuss a cost-saving idea with her at lunch. . . . The next day it's in a memo to the boss, signed by her! You:

a. Feel mildly annoyed—doesn't she have a mind of her own?—but too sorry for her to make an issue of it.

b. *Like her*—she's a constant reminder of how *brilliant* you are!

c. Quietly make sure everybody knows it was *you* who originated those ideas.

d. Take her aside and ask her to stop borrowing from you—perhaps she hadn't realized she was doing it!

12. A man you find obnoxious has been coming on strong, although you've repeatedly refused to go out with him. He's tried the bribe ("I'll rent a Rolls, baby, it'll be caviar and champagne") . . . the threat ("If you don't see me, I'll stay on your doorstep all night") . . . and now he wants to *shame* you into seeing him ("Listen, doll, just because I'm not handsome or one of those young kids, you think you're too *good* for me, right?"). You:
a. Say, "Right, I *am* too good for you, so please go away now."
b. Calmly tell him to leave you alone and you mean it.
c. Invent a large, jealous lover who doesn't allow anyone else in your life.
d. Decide you'll go out with him *once*—anything to get rid of him. . . .
e. Don't have the problem because at the outset you told him, "I think you're an utter darling and would like to consider you a good friend . . . but I could *never* get romantic with you—sorry!"

13. Your dearest friend betrays a secret she swore never to reveal (your love techniques, bank statement, existence of those skinny-dipping photos from last summer). You:
a. Make a vow to yourself to "leak" one of *her* most damaging secrets.
b. Break off the friendship—at least for a while.
c. Tell her you're disappointed in her and resolve not to tell her any more really personal facts.
d. Complain, but somehow let the same thing happen again. She's so much fun to confide

in, you can never resist—even *knowing* what will happen.
e. Feel put-upon for a week or so, then forget it—having secrets is silly anyway.

14. The man you love hits you—really hits you—not once, not twice, but on *three* different occasions. Do you break off with him?
a. He *wouldn't* hit you three times—you'd be gone after the first.
b. Perhaps, but no more so than over any *other* form of serious disagreement. . . . Sometimes, expressing anger physically is good for a relationship.
c. No—you'd hit him back!
d. Yes, although reluctantly. A man that violent is probably mentally disturbed and needs help.
e. Not necessarily. First, you'd think about whether you're provoking him or not understanding his needs.

SCORING: Find the point value for each of your answers, then add them all up.

1.	a.1	b.4	c.5	d.3	e.2
2.	a.3	b.4	c.5	d.1	e.2
3.	a.5	b.1	c.2	d.4	e.3
4.	a.4	b.2	c.5	d.1	e.3
5.	a.2	b.1	c.3	d.5	e.4
6.	a.1	b.2	c.3	d.4	
7.	a.1	b.2	c.5	d.3	e.4
8.	a.1	b.5	c.2	d.3	e.4
9.	a.4	b.2	c.1	d.3	
10.	a.2	b.1	c.3	d.4	
11.	a.2	b.3	c.1	d.4	
12.	a.5	b.4	c.2	d.1	e.3
13.	a.4	b.5	c.3	d.1	e.2
14.	a.2	b.4	c.5	d.3	e.1

58-66 points: You take *zero* guff—no one is ever going to accuse *you* of slipping through life unnoticed! You are a leader. When everyone else is afraid, you speak up. You'll stop a man on the street from beating his dog . . . or lie down in front of a bulldozer to save a grove of trees. In social situations you accept no slights or meannesses. Take care not to act too hastily, though: examine the situation carefully to make sure a wrong was really done, and *intended,* before you explode. You have a fatal attraction for weak men, who seek in you what they lack. Avoid them—you need a man as strong as you are!

48-57 points: Knowing you have a vicious temper which shouldn't be vented indiscriminately, you repress until you feel enough unequivocal guff has been handed you, then you *blow up!* Figuratively speaking, you're the type most likely to be found with a body at your feet and a smoking revolver in your hand. Never one to forgive a slight, wrong or insult, you smolder until vengeance is obtained. Men find your combination of cool exterior and seething inner volcano a real turn-on. You're probably a *tigress* in bed, where you can *always* act out what you feel. Generally you get good treatment in life, since most people sense you're simply *not* to be trifled with.

38-47 points: Yours is the most *normal* score: when you have a grievance, you make it known in a constructive manner aimed at solving the problem. You don't like to be hurt, neither do you like hurting others, which makes you able to see a situation from everybody's viewpoint. Relaxed and unresentful, you expect fair treatment and usually get it; when you don't, you simply speak up. People do take advantage of you in one respect, however: you're so sensible and fair-minded they're always coming to you for advice. Extremes in men (wild-eyed neurotics, incipient Hitlers) stay out of your life . . . except when they feel they need you as ballast against their particular form of madness. The really *good* men adore you—you have so much to offer!

29-37 points: Basically, you're very loving and act on the assumption that everyone else is, too. When someone returns your kindness with treachery or callousness, you're shocked and amazed. Too sweet and sensitive to be very good at angry self-assertion, you *do* often find yourself being exploited. Your solution? Simply avoid aggressive rotters. With so many nice folks around, why bother with them? Your best social milieu is one that appreciates but doesn't try to take advantage of your generosity. Men adore you because you're so *giving,* but stay away from lovers who need you too much. You should be sheltered and protected, not leaned on. Just because you're sweet, don't think you're not being *effective*—you are!

28 points or less: You're unbelievable! You can lend someone lunch money every day for a month and never ask to be paid back . . . never *care* . . . and not even be mad at yourself. You'll bring chicken soup to your enemies when they're sick in bed, buy things you don't need because you don't want to hurt the salesman's feelings, and be a loyal and devoted wife to a sadist with twelve mistresses. Most people adore you (with good reason!), but is that really enough? Too bad you don't live in the fourteenth century, because then you'd have a chance to become a saint. . . . Since this is 1980, however, why not try to be just a little firmer with people around you—sometimes it's kinder to say *no.*

How Daring Are You?

LOUISE MORGAN

Are you a bold adventuress? Or a bit of a turtle, always drawing in your tender parts and shutting interesting experiences *out*? You *need* a measure of daring, you know, to extract the pleasure and the *juice* from life. Not that you have to drive in the Indy 500 or tumble out of the ionosphere in a parachute —what's being measured here is the punch in your *social* style. To find out whether you're bound by convention and routine or live joyously in the *moment*, take this little test. And be *honest*—our answers here are *not* as simple as they may seem!

SECTION I Mark the following statements True or False.

1. Friends are rarely critical of my behavior. _____

2. People who've met me casually generally remember my name and a few salient facts of my life on next meeting. _____

3. I've made perhaps *two* good new friends in the past three years. _____

4. I almost never cry. _____

5. I'd rather be promoted in the company I work for *now* than look for a new job. _____

6. Friends usually call me more often than I call them. _____

7. I own one dress in shimmering turquoise or fire-engine red. _____

8. I'd *adore* taking a year or two off from my job and just drifting. _____

9. I feel disturbed if friends drop by unannounced. _____

10. I love opening my mailbox or answering a ringing phone. _____

11. People say I'm a terrific dancer. _____

12. I'm attracted to men who are very *different* from me. _____

13. I'm very easily *bored.* ____

14. I've been wearing my hair the same way for the past two years. ____

15. I think people who devote lots of time to "hobbies" are hiding out from real commitment. ____

SECTION II   Choose the most appropriate response to each question.

1. You are redecorating your bedroom when your lover suggests a huge circular bed and mirrored ceilings. You—
a. Agree that might be fun, but worry about what your *mother* will think of such lurid decor on her next visit.
b. Immediately phone the decorator to get estimates.
c. Wonder a little about the boyfriend—you feel people who must have "props" are often compensating for an *under*active sex drive.
d. Decorate your boudoir more sedately but agree to spend the next weekend at an X-rated motel!

2. While driving in the country with a friend, you suddenly discover a gorgeous roadside waterfall. You—
a. Immediately suggest a hike into the woods beyond.
b. Drive to the nearest town, get a hiker's map and *then* take off.
c. Plan to return and picnic there some day when you're more adequately *equipped.*
d. Ruefully leave the pretty site—you haven't *time* to linger now.

3. If suddenly rich, you would buy—
a. A thoroughbred race horse.
b. An ocean-going sailboat.
c. A perfect little brownstone.
d. A collection of precious gems.

4. An attractive man approaches you on the street and in elegantly accented English, says he thinks you are very beautiful. You—
a. Smile prettily, but walk on by.
b. Talk to him for a minute or two. If he seems a sensible sort, jot down your home phone number.
c. Politely tell him he's brightened *your* day, too.
d. Chat flirtatiously for a bit, then suggest he call you at your office for lunch next week.

5. You would describe your closets friends as—
a. Buoyantly extroverted just like you—you can't stand people who bring you *down.*
b. Appealing in lots of *different* ways—your taste in people is *eclectic.*
c. Solidly in your *class.* Intellectually and socially you've a good deal in common.
d. Sufficiently generous, gifted, and bright to *add* to your life.

6. Lovers frequently compliment you on being—
a. Intelligent, great to talk to.
b. Attentive and lovingly concerned with them.
c. Dynamite in bed.
d. Great-looking.

7. You'd have the most difficulty living happily in—
a. A hideously furnished apartment.
b. A place that's just too *small.*

c. An apartment in a horrible neighborhood.
d. Digs shared with a horrendously sloppy roommate.

8. Your world view might be best described as—
a. Intelligent/cautious.
b. Romantic/optimistic.
c. Cheerful/realistic.

9. You would most enjoy a vacation spent—
a. In some outrageously *exotic* locale . . . Tahiti, say, or Nepal.
b. Engaged in some wonderfully engrossing activity. Glacier skiing in the Alps or scuba diving in the Caribbean would definitely turn you on.
c. At a French château or Italian villa in the company of somebody most distingué.
d. At a fabulous beach resort, lazily sunbathing by day, disco dancing at night.

10. A man you adore but have been very unsure of impetuously proposes matrimony. You—
a. Tell him such decisions aren't made in a flash. You'll give him an answer after some consideration.
b. Say you'd love to, but ask him to propose again next week. You must be sure he really *wants* to marry you.
c. Say yes, and head directly to the nearest justice of the peace.
d. Are thrilled but *incredulous*—by tomorrow, he'll certainly have changed his mind.

11. After a difficult day you prefer to unwind by—
a. Enjoying a lovely supper all alone.
b. Running a mile, showering, collapsing into bed.
c. Having dinner out with friends.
d. Inviting over a very *special* person, someone in whose company you can totally *relax*.

12. You'd be most pleased by a man who brought you—
a. First-class tickets for two to Paris!
b. Something special and precious from Cartier.
c. Romantic surprises—a dozen pink roses for no reason at all, champagne and caviar on Saturday morning. Brie and French bread for Sunday supper.
d. Gifts that show he's been paying *attention*—the Halston jump suit you mentioned liking, tapes of all your favorite songs.

13. Your dashing boss might, with slight *encouragement*, also become a lover. You—
a. Are quietly flirtatious. You don't come on *too* flagrantly, though.
b. Go all *out* to entrance him.
c. Get nervous—sex and the office are a *disastrous* mix.
d. Wait for *him* to make a move.

14. An attractive man met briefly on a plane or at a resort, has insisted that you call if you're ever in his home city. When business takes you there, you—
a. Phone him right away. No better way to know a city than to see it with a friendly native!
b. Call, but expect him to have probably forgotten his offer. If this seems the case, you plan to sign off *fast*.
c. Refrain from phoning unless you grow *very* fidgety and bored.
d. Don't call at all—invitations like that are never *really* meant.

15. Your most idyllic lovers' Sunday would be spent—

a. Noodling about in bed.

b. Seeking out romantic trysting spots—the perfect little café, a gorgeous and deserted beach.

c. Hiking together in the woods, making love on a bed of pine needles!

d. In decadently *lazy* luxury. You'd lunch at an *important* restaurant, browse through an ultrachic gallery, dance at the most glamorous club in town.

SCORING: Give yourself points as follows:

Section I

1.	True 0	False 5
2.	True 5	False 0
3.	True 0	False 5
4.	True 0	False 5
5.	True 0	False 5
6.	True 5	False 0
7.	True 5	False 0
8.	True 5	False 0
9.	True 0	False 5
10.	True 5	False 0
11.	True 5	False 0
12.	True 5	False 0
13.	True 0	False 5
14.	True 0	False 5
15.	True 0	False 5

Section II

1.	a.2	b.4	c.1	d.3
2.	a.4	b.3	c.2	d.1
3.	a.3	b.4	c.1	d.2
4.	a.1	b.4	c.2	d.3
5.	a.4	b.3	c.1	d.2
6.	a.2	b.3	c.4	d.1
7.	a.4	b.3	c.1	d.2
8.	a.2	b.4	c.3	
9.	a.4	b.3	c.2	d.1
10.	a.3	b.1	c.4	d.2
11.	a.2	b.1	c.4	d.3
12.	a.4	b.1	c.3	d.2
13.	a.3	b.4	c.1	d.2
14.	a.4	b.3	c.2	d.1
15.	a.2	b.3	c.4	d.1

If you scored from 115 to 135 points, you are a "*bon vivant*"; from 80 to 114 points, a "gay charmer"; from 60 to 79 points, a "careful lady"; under 60 points, a "quiet mouse." Read below for a description of your "type."

Bon vivant: You are recklessly, passionately in love with all kinds of experience and seek to jam every day of your life with truly *memorable* moments. Ebullient, charming, and so unpredictable, you're the daring girl who's hardly *ever* conservative or shy. One word of caution, though—in your eagerness to gobble life *up*, you may tread on the feelings of people who are somewhat *less* impulsive. You haven't time to waste with mousey companions and don't trouble to disguise your boredom when they're around. Try to be kinder, please, and to think, too, about subduing that lust for life just a touch. Your indiscriminate appetite for experience might get you into *serious* mischief one day soon.

Gay charmer: You're very nearly as daring and open to experience as the *bon vivant,* but, unlike her, you tend to be neither rude *nor* reckless. You temper your craving for experience with sound good sense, stay well away from danger, and treat people whose temperament is more timid than yours with sweet *understanding*. You view each experience life offers as a wondrous gift, but are not so grabby as to insist on a bonanza *every* day. Congratulations—you're the spontaneous yet sensible girl who is always up for the right *kind* of adventure.

Careful lady: You're not quite as jauntily daring as you could be, especially considering how blessedly confident you are in other ways. For some reason you *distrust* whatever is spontaneous and unplanned, and while this caution often serves you well (a get-ahead girl, you're likely to earn and marry well), lack of spontaneity does deprive you of many of life's lustier pleasures. Relax a bit . . . you'll have more fun with friends and lovers if you loosen up, and you'll find they'll like *you* better too.

Quiet mouse: You are so busy scouting out possible danger that you miss many of life's *most* enchanting times. And you'll never build up wobbly self-confidence so long as you elect the society of companions who are even *more* fearful and habit ridden than you. Try cultivating a few flamboyant easy-going friends (their happy madness is *catching*). And try, too, to break free of the spiritless little rituals that keep you "safe" but also boringly penned *in*. Take small steps at first . . . bike to your office instead of boarding the No. 7 bus, buy some outrageous sunglasses, then work up to a love affair, say, with a really intriguing stranger. You need to *free* imprisoned impulses if you're to get as much excitement out of life as you *should*.

How Generous Are You?

BARBARA JOHNSTON, PH.D.

This quiz is designed to measure your *emotional* generosity—are you overly liberal with praise or a scrimper; quick to take joy in somebody else's good fortune or grudging? (Some money questions are included since emotional *largess,* or the lack of it, is often reflected by fiscal maneuverings.) Imagine yourself in the following situations and choose the response you would most *typically* make. Do be candid, and don't pick "good girl" answers unless you really feel that way. (Besides, "good" answers can be "bad." Every healthy person needs *some* emotional selfishness—which makes our quiz less "simple" than it might seem.)

1. You have no steady lover, and feel the pinch of loneliness. Meanwhile, a good girlfriend has begun to date a lovely man and no longer has time for *you*. You feel:
a. Angry, and less inclined to be such a good friend to the girl. If situations had been reversed, you would have still had time for *her*.
b. Happy that somebody else has found a good man. You feel encouraged, and think your luck may change as quickly as hers.
c. A little envious . . . why couldn't it have been *you?*
d. That your wretchedness is somehow made *worse* by comparison with her good fortune.

2. You are invited to lunch by an attractive male business friend, and another couple unexpectedly joins your table. The girl is a real beauty; her looks upstage yours entirely. You *had* planned to flirt your way to a closer relationship with your business date; now you:
a. Feel your plans have been spoiled. You mumble through lunch, curse your luck, and eat more than usual.

b. Are a little cross that this knockout had to show up, but adjust to the situation.

c. Are awed into shy silence. You don't feel the situation is *unjust,* but why try to force your date to pay attention to you when this glorious creature is present?

d. Don't feel your position has altered much; gorgeous though she is, the girl is the *other* guy's date.

3. You're sharing a European vacation with a girl who's independently wealthy, while you've had to work all year to save for two weeks of luxury. She suggests picking up the bill for a seashore side trip you've spent together and you:

a. *Accept!* She's frankly rich and you're *not,* so why quarrel?

b. Accept a bit guiltily. You'd rather pay your own way, but she insists and, rather than fuss, you agree.

c. Accept, then reciprocate by buying her a nice present. Even though your gift isn't as costly as the hotel bill, you feel the balance has been "evened up."

d. Accept, but feel like little-poor-girl.

4. A former lover (*he* dropped *you*) finds a new girlfriend who is both pretty and successful. You:

a. Realize he was pretty heady for you, and wish you had as many fabulous qualities as his new love.

b. Find yourself "inspecting" the girl for flaws ... measuring *her* inadequacies against *yours.*

c. Cannot quite be *pleased* that he's happy, but try hard to push the affair out of your mind, and not compare yourself to her.

d. Can't help feeling angry, but you'd be even more wretched if the girl were ugly and

unemployed ... then you'd have to wonder if you were an even *worse* catastrophe.

5. A generous genie offers you one of the following wishes. You choose:

a. Immense wealth.

b. Bliss in love.

c. Fame and power.

d. Happiness for yourself and those you love.

e. To be born again and start all *over.*

6. A close girlfriend has qualities you admire, and must admit, are sometimes lacking in yourself. (She is better tempered, more hard-working, possibly prettier, and in some ways smarter than you.) When her good qualities are most glowingly apparent, you feel:

a. Resentment pangs ... you don't enjoy being shown up by comparison.

b. Inadequate. Seeing her makes you realize how far *you* have to go.

c. Particularly warm and affectionate toward her. Those qualities are what made you choose her as a friend in the *first* place.

d. Happy that such a gifted girl has chosen to make you her friend.

7. A colleague at the office is promoted, and you honestly feel you deserved the advance more than she. You:

a. Feel acutely resentful toward her for a week or two, then grow more cordial—it wasn't *her* fault the boss was unfair.

b. Think guiltily about all those nights you *didn't* stay late at the office. ... If you'd been more conscientious, the job might have been yours.

c. *Cannot* squash bad feelings. Though you try to like the girl, she remains a reminder of *your* failure.

d. Accept the situation, but notice that sometimes you're a bit *testier* around her than other co-workers.

8. A brother or sister is happily married, but you haven't yet found a love. You:

a. Remind yourself that your brother's or sister's needs always *were* less complicated than your own; it is not too surprising that he/she has found someone before you have.

b. Are happy to have some new "family," and make every effort to relate warmly to your in-law.

c. Feel somewhat wistful that your sibling's marriage has reduced the intimacy you and she (he) used to share.

d. Try to think constructively about what quality your brother or sister has that you *lack*—figuring this out could help you make a happy match some day.

e. Feel a little sad when around the two of them; their perfect "togetherness" makes you feel almost isolated.

9. Your lover has a taste for some in-bed activity you don't care for (nothing perverted or kinky, just not *arousing*). You:

a. Indulge him, and pretend to enjoy this bit of eroticism as much as he.

b. Go along with the program, but prefer not to fake enjoyment.

c. Feel guilty about not sharing his taste. Sometimes you even initiate this particular act, so he'll be *sure* not to know it leaves you indifferent.

d. Feel that doing what doesn't turn you on would be hypocritical and damaging to your relationship.

10. At Christmas you:

a. Usually give presents to those with whom you have a "give and take" arrangement—you and they always exchange gifts.

b. Throw in a few surprise gifts for new friends, though you know they might not reciprocate.

c. Would enjoy buying impulse gifts, but feel you might embarrass a friend by a surprise; she or he might regret not having given *you* a gift.

d. Wish the whole gift-giving business would be abolished, except for children. The hectic rush of shopping really upsets you.

11. Which of the following best describes your attitude toward entertaining at home?

a. Sometimes painful, since parties often misfire, but worth doing *anyhow*.

b. A chore . . . you entertain when you *must*, for professional or family reason, but feel a hostess has too many *other* worries to enjoy her own party.

c. It's all simply good fun.

d. Intimidating. You feel painfully responsible if your guests don't have a good time.

12. If you had only one living parent and he or she were to become seriously ill and require the care of a round-the-clock nurse, you would:

a. *Want* to have the parent with you if at all possible. You believe old people should live and die at *home*.

b. Find the best nursing home you could afford and visit often.

c. Unhesitatingly discharge your part of the responsibility, but try to make sure other close relatives do their share as well.

d. Acknowledge that you *must* take in the ill parent, though this may seem to disrupt your own life.

13. Which of the following sets of attributes attracts you most to a man?
a. Money, status, and power.
b. Intelligence and imagination.
c. His willingness to love *you*.
d. The ability to respect your privacy and independence.
e. Good looks and a passionate nature.

14. Your attitude toward having children is best described as:
a. Negative. You feel motherhood limits a woman's aspirations, and can't see how the so-called "joys" could ever compensate for the disadvantages.
b. Ambiguous. You *might* want a child someday, but worry that this would close off other options to you.
c. Eager. You think children still provide life's most fulfilling joys, for women *and* men.
d. Uncertain—mainly because you suspect you're not suited to motherhood: What if you were overly protective or demanding and raised a total *neurotic!*

15. A friend asks to borrow a book you are in the process of reading. You:
a. Feel embarrassed by the situation, and quickly say yes without mentioning you have been reading the book yourself.
b. Say you'll give her the book next week— that *you're* right in the middle of it now.
c. Agree to lend her the book, then feel angry with her for asking and with *yourself* for granting the request.
d. Simply say, "Sorry, I'm reading it myself." You don't like lending books, since they are so rarely returned, and are glad to have an honest excuse not to lose this one.

SCORING KEY: ×'s indicate the emotional scrimper who is a little tight with both her time and her love.
○ answers are too unselfish, indicating a tendency toward martyrdom.
△'s are answers that signal a *balanced* generosity.
□'s are miserly responses, revealing the emotional hoarder.

	a	b	c	d	e
1.	□	△	△	×	
2.	□	×	○	△	
3.	□	○	△	×	
4.	○	×	△	×	
5.	□	△	×	△	○
6.	□	×	△	○	
7.	△	○	□	×	
8.	×	△	×	○	△
9.	△	×	○	□	
10.	×	△	○	□	
11.	△	×	△	○	
12.	△	×	×	○	
13.	×	△	○	□	△
14.	□	△	○	△	
15.	○	△	×	□	

SCORING: What's important is the category that contains the *majority* of your responses. Almost everybody who takes this test gives one or more answers drawn from each category— even the most wonderfully generous girl will be unexpectedly miserly in a certain area of her life, just as the emotional hoarder will be uncharacteristically generous at times. If your answers are split more or less evenly between one category of response and another, this means you share traits of both character types. Some common mixes: A girl who scores mostly △'s (signaling a healthy generosity) will also choose more than a few ○'s (too selfless), while a preponderance of ×'s (stingy) often goes with a good share of □ (miser) responses. Sometimes, though, the too-selfless girl finds she also chooses quite a few *miserly* answers; this may mean she resents her role of martyr and compensates by being grabby at times. We'll outline only what the four major types indicate about personality; estimate your own *personal* balance.

○'s—**The Emotional Spendthrift.** A preponderance of ○ responses (9 to 14) means you are *too* generous and apt to give away what more properly ought to be kept for *yourself*. An ○ personality isn't *genuinely* giving, however. Her tendency to be overly selfless is motivated by *fear* rather than love. She feels she can only gain the world's approval by sacrificing her own interests to those of other people. Sadly, she is wrong. People feel uncomfortable around an emotional spendthrift, and this uneasiness is apt to translate into resentment. Such a reaction confounds the too-selfless girl. She is unaware that her profligate giving produces guilt not pleasure in the recipients.

△'s—**The Truly Generous Girl.** Mostly △ answers (11 to 15) show you are able to give because of an emotional abundance *within*, rather than out of timidity, like the spendthrift. You have a balanced emotional budget! The truly generous girl is like a wealthy country. Her natural resources are vast, and she can, therefore, afford to give without risking depletion. Sometimes, however, the generous girl is misunderstood by people who, not naturally giving themselves, suspect her of "ulterior motives." These people can't understand a person who gives just because it *feels* good, and not because of some unexpressed desire for hidden profits. If you picked mostly △'s, though, you may be capable of *forgiving* stingier souls for their lack of empathy. You *deserve* admiration, even if you don't always get it.

×'s—**The Emotional Scrimper.** An × personality (11 to 14) is often *capable* of generosity, but she's also afraid of it. She's the emotional equivalent of a Depression child, who, no matter how affluent she becomes in later life, can't forget the poverties of her childhood. The scrimper would often like to be generous, but she fears that she may accidentally give away some vital quality that's necessary for her *own* survival. Usually the scrimper knew emotional "hard times" as a child, and these unhappy memories prevent her from being a generous adult. The × personality is characteristically erratic in her generosity—if she feels "safe" —that is, if no threat is near—she can afford to give, but when menaced by any rival, or by "dangerous" circumstances, she closes up and keeps everything for herself!

□'s—**The Hoarder.** The personality who consistently (9 to 11) chooses □ responses has a damaged sense of self. She, like the overly giving girl, is ruled by fear—but in her case, fear ,keeps a *miserly* hold on her emotions. This girl incessantly compares herself to other people, and is happy only when she is *clearly* superior to them. She manages to retain this sense of superiority only by attributing the basest motives to those around her. She sees threats where there are none, and faults where they don't exist. And why *should* she be generous to the nasty, self-seeking people by whom (as she views it), she is constantly surrounded. If you are in this category, take care. The price the hoader pays for her faulty and defensive view of humanity can be steep. She may *appear* to get through life without damage (the hoarder is nothing if not careful), but she is a prime target for stress diseases, and is rarely capable of happy relationships.

Exploring Emotional Depths

Feelings are the very *stuff* of life. Your emotional *reaction* to events often matters more than what's actually taking place. If feelings go out of control, however, *you're* the loser. Copers manage their emotions first—competence follows from that.

This chapter explores and describes your particular emotional make-up. Do you feel deeply and easily or are you overly constrained? Learn in our first quiz whether to ease up or *tighten* control. Then find out if gauzy romance filters your picture of life or if you're a sharp-eyed cynic. (Both ways of viewing reality bring *advantages*.) Next, discover how contented you are with your life's progress—you can *be* happy and hardly notice it. Isn't that surprising?

How about measuring your relative humanitarianism? Perhaps you're more ruthless (or sweetly altruistic) than you know. Maturity is another quality that will be assessed here—are you overly-grown-up and missing all the fun, or so much the child you'll never *un*scramble your messy life? Finally, are you so suspicious you hardly make a single spontaneous move? Guileless innocents may get *taken* more frequently than the worldly cynics, but they often have more *fun!*

What's Your Emotional Style?

LOUISE MORGAN

We're all *emotional* to some degree—this quiz is designed to establish how you choose to *vent* compelling emotional forces. Styles vary, you see. Some of us no sooner experience joy, sorrow, jealousy than we follow up the feeling with *action*. Others are more reticent, perhaps not trusting gut urges entirely (intense feelings can cause trouble) or believing it wrong and weak to allow emotions to govern behavior. Which type are you, restrained or spontaneous? Answer the following questions to find out, and remember, one personality type isn't necessarily better than another . . . each style of reacting can lead to happiness—as well as to hurt, alas. So do be *honest!*

1. You've split with a lover or mate and the breakup was not easy for you. Next day, you:

a. Stay home from the office, weep, and drink endless cups of coffee. You must *grieve* over this loss.

b. Go to work and labor even more diligently than usual. You dare not give yourself the chance to go to pieces.

c. Appear at the office in a bedraggled state, but actually find yourself *forgetting,* if only for minutes at a time, what has happened. The distractions of the job take your mind away from your "tragedy."

d. Go to work, but drift through the day in a daze. You cannot quite *believe* the two of you are quits.

2. You meet an impressive new man, one who appears to fit all your "specs" for an important love. You:

a. Immediately begin to suspect that he's *not* all he seems . . . you're careful to check any premature fantasies of bliss.

b. Congratulate yourself on meeting a winner, and hope *very* much that he calls soon.

c. Don't even *attempt* to contain your enthusiasm— the phone rings, you pray it's him.

d. Think he'll call, but are almost *afraid* to expect he will!

3. You phone your closest girlfriend:
a. About once a week or whenever something special happens.
b. Nearly every day—you can always use her viewpoint on some dilemma, or else just want to see how she *is*.
c. Generally, a few days after she last called you.
d. Whenever you want to *see* her for drinks, a movie, or a visit. It's not your style to just phone and chat.

4. When you were growing up, your mother was:
a. A worrier . . . she loved you fiercely but tended to overprotect.
b. A pussycat . . . always there when you needed her, but never *hovering*. You made many of your own decisions from an early age.
c. Loving, yes, but rather too wrapped up in her own life (or in your father) to be over-concerned with her children.
d. A perfectionist . . . she expected a lot from her children and generally inspired it.

5. You turn in an important piece of work, then:
a. Worry ceaselessly until you get some feedback. Try though you may to stay cool, you will possibly go in and *ask* about it after a reasonable wait.
b. Feel embarrassed if you brush by the boss in the hall. He may have thought what you did inadequate but is too kind to say so.
c. Wait in *relative* calm for the work to be judged . . . there is nothing you can do now to change the outcome.
d. Put yesterday's work almost entirely out of mind, and focus on making today's count.

6. You've quarreled with a lover, and the two of you have bitterly returned to separate apartments. Once home, you:
a. Have a nightcap and go to sleep. You'll resume the "discussion" *next* time you meet.
b. Call him to say you're suffering and to ask how *he's* feeling.
c. Review the course of your entire affair as you lay your curls on the pillow. Possibly he is *not* the darling you thought he was.
d. Cry yourself to sleep. You can't bear the fight you've just had!

7. If fired from a job that has mattered deeply to you, you would:
a. Plan a way to prove to the person who did the firing that he was *wrong*—becoming a sought-after free-lancer or getting hired by a more prestigious firm will show him!
b. Begin somewhat to doubt your own competence. Were you in beyond your depth? Ought you, perhaps, to try for a more modest job next time?
c. Coolly review your performance. If you find some justification in the firing, resolve never to be so stupid again. If the boss's judgment seems wrong, determine never to work for such a dumb *person* again.
d. Be shaken, naturally, but you take consolation in knowing you did do your *best*. If you didn't please Mr. Big, perhaps that's *his* problem.

8. You're alone on the streets at night and an angry drunk stumbles by. He seems too out-of-it to hurt you, still, he *is* menacing. You:
a. Cross the street and walk home no more swiftly than usual.
b. Take off your high heels and *run*.
c. Bite your lip and walk on, trying to be *ignorable*.

d. Walk to the nearest phone booth and tell the police there's a rather menacing person on Sloane Street.

9. You are having ten people to dinner, five more than you've entertained before. An hour before they're due to arrive, you:
a. Begin to do rather odd things like arranging the top shelf of your closet even though the canapés aren't finished.
b. Think that probably no one will come. Actually, you'd be most relieved if they *did* stay away!
c. Fuss endlessly with the flowers and hors d'oeuvre, even though they're perfect.
d. Pour yourself a drink, take to your tub, and relax!

10. Of the following classic fictional heroines, you identify most closely with:
a. Catherine in *Wuthering Heights*
b. Melanie in *Gone With the Wind*
c. Natasha in *War and Peace*
d. Jane in *Jane Eyre*

11. When you look back, your past seems to you:
a. Less than might have been. In the future, you'll be more adventurous.
b. A subtly shaded mosaic . . . probably there's been a pattern, though *you* can't discern one.
c. Slow, steady progress toward your present. You are more or less where you'd hoped to be five years ago.
d. Happy, sad, baffling, funny . . . all the things that life must *be*.

12. You determine to give up some habit you've cherished but believe is *bad* for you (smoking, eating sweets, drinking twelve cups of coffee a day). During the first few days of deprivation, you:
a. Guard vigilantly against even the *thought* of the longed-for but forsworn treat. Nonetheless, you grow cranky and irritable.
b. Think and talk incessantly about how much you want an éclair or a smoke . . . even *dream* about the forbidden bonbon.
c. Find yourself in a mild depression.
d. Endure the agony by reminding yourself you're on the right path. One day soon, you'll find yourself not even missing the specific treat.

13. There are two men in your life and you'd like to decide on one or the other. You:
a. Wait to see which man wants and cherishes *you* the most, then probably choose him.
b. Worry and fret . . . you can't know for certain which one is more desirable, and this is a *very* important decision.
c. Review each man's behavior carefully and try to make a meaningful and *sensible* choice.
d. Listen to your emotions . . . go with the one who makes you feel happiest.

14. You feel a sibling or parent has behaved toward you in a hurtful way. Your response is to:
a. Fester until the issue is resolved. You cannot *rest* when out of harmony with your family.
b. Remember all the sweet things the offender has done, and try to forgive. Not even family can be expected always to be kind.
c. Write the spiteful one out of your life for a short time. Why accept behavior from family that you wouldn't tolerate in a friend?
d. Feel terribly *betrayed* . . . if you can't trust your loved ones, whom can you count on?

15. A saleslady has waited on two customers who came to the counter after you, and you've begun to suspect deliberate malice. You:

a. Leave without saying a word, vowing never to return.

b. Finally ask the girl what she thinks she's *doing.* You are angry and can *articulate* your wrath.

c. Say, "Miss, I believe I'm next," in a very firm tone that would be hard to ignore.

d. Leave the store but not before contacting the manager to tell him about the situation.

16. A girlfriend with whom you have a dinner date stands you up. Next morning, she phones to explain that a man she's wildly interested in called at the last minute and, though she *tried* to get you, you'd apparently already left. Surely, you'll understand. You:

a. Blast her . . . you find such rudeness infuriating and tell her so. Next day, though, you may relent—after all, you *might* have done the same in her place if the man was *very* desirable.

b. Pretend to accept her apology, but finish the conversation seething with unexpressed resentment. You privately resolve that you and she will be friends no longer.

c. Explain, as graciously as possible, how very *un*gracious you believe she's been.

d. Ice her . . . without saying much, you let her know that further phone calls will be unwelcome.

17. Your regular boyfriend spots you out with another man on a night when you'd *said* you were going over to Connie's to visit. When he calls, after a delay of a few days, you:

a. Trepidatiously wait for him to bring up the incident and, when he does, guiltily crumble into apologies.

b. Explain quietly that your arrangement is, after all, pretty loose, and you don't feel accountable to him.

c. Take the offensive . . . remind *him* of the time he was due at your place at eight and showed up, completely tanked, at two!

d. Try to joke him out of his ill humor: Yes, you were wrong and, indeed, you got *caught,* but that's no reason to chuck a basically happy relationship, is it?

18. A rival at the office sneakily and rather cleverly manages to garner credit for *your* work. You:

a. Openly declare war. If she wants to get nasty, you can be even *more* so, and you tell her as much.

b. Outmaneuver her . . . even while pretending not really to notice what she's done, you cultivate powerful office allies who will make life hard on *her.*

c. Stay out of her way . . . the office is a place to work, not fight, and if she's so insecure as to need applause for others' work, then let her have it.

d. Talk to her as openly and as amiably as you can, suggesting she's talented—so why be sneaky? Without *condoning* what she's done (she won't steal your praise again, right?), you'd like to be friends.

SCORING: Circle your answer for each question on the grid:

1.	a.1	b.2	c.3	d.4	**10.**	a.1	b.2	c.3	d.4
2.	a.2	b.3	c.1	d.4	**11.**	a.4	b.1	c.2	d.3
3.	a.3	b.1	c.4	d.2	**12.**	a.2	b.1	c.4	d.3
4.	a.1	b.3	c.4	d.2	**13.**	a.4	b.1	c.2	d.3
5.	a.1	b.4	c.2	d.3	**14.**	a.1	b.3	c.2	d.4
6.	a.3	b.1	c.2	d.4	**15.**	a.4	b.1	c.3	d.2
7.	a.1	b.4	c.2	d.3	**16.**	a.1	b.4	c.3	d.2
8.	a.3	b.1	c.4	d.2	**17.**	a.4	b.2	c.1	d.3
9.	a.1	b.4	c.2	d.3	**18.**	a.1	b.2	c.4	d.3

Review the choices you've circled to see what pattern emerges. If you have a preponderance of "1" answers, you are Emotionally Assertive; mostly "2s" indicate an Emotionally Controlled personality; a majority of "3s" means you're Emotionally Balanced; while "4" answers indicate the Emotionally Timid girl. Now, read the profile of your "type," below.

1. The Emotionally Assertive Girl: Feelings are *the* most compelling force in your life—you don't even attempt to resist their sway. No sooner are assertive girls touched by a ripple of feeling than decisive action follows! And you're equally determined that the entire *world* yield to the force of your powerful spirit. Among your virtues, count a positive, often radiantly dynamic and *strong* nature . . . but, alas, you also suffer from emotional willfulness. Sometimes those rash actions lead to fatefully unhappy consequences, and you may grow physically *ill* if inner needs are thwarted. You'd do well to at least *try* to moderate those insistent feelings and learn to tolerate a little frustration.

2. The Emotionally Controlled Girl: Your emotions are as strong as those of the Assertive Girl but, unlike her, you've an even fiercer need *not* to allow emotions to pull moods out of control. However, efforts to organize your life so as to *contain* vigorous emotional drives don't *always* succeed! Stubborn feelings surface anyway, often in the form of mysterious spells of irritability or psychosomatic illness. Though you're a forceful and admirably disciplined person, you find it difficult ever to fully relax (unruly feelings might just take *hold*) and may tend, too, to be rigidly intolerant. Try allowing emotions just a touch of leeway, and see if you aren't happier and more accepting. True, that control is monumentally impressive, but you tend to ask too *much* of yourself.

3. The Emotionally Balanced Girl: Congratulations . . . of all the psychological types outlined here, you obtain the deepest pleasure from life. Emotions are powerful, you realize, and to be respected; but while giving them proper credit, you're also realistic enough to know that *your* feelings don't rule the world. An emotional grown-up, you tend to be at harmony with inner needs and with other people—and that deep-rooted composure acts as an awesome magnet. Paradoxically, though less *insistent* than the two previously described types, you're more likely to *get* what you want! Your *un*threatening deportment inspires others to generosity.

4. The Emotionally Timid Girl: You feel as potently as other girls, but suffer from a sense that the world is titanically *more* powerful, and fear that to bare delicate feelings is to see them crushed. This timidity leads you to turn emotions inward, refusing to express what you truly feel. Price paid for this denial: frequent bouts of gloom and depression. On the plus side, though, you rarely frustrate yourself by pressing importunate emotional demands on others and may even achieve a certain serene acceptance of things as they are. To be free of melancholy, though, you must learn to *trust* emotions more. Try to loosen up . . . you'll find that everybody else really *isn't* wickedly intent on annihilating your feelings!

How Romantic Are You?

LOUISE MORGAN

Romance is tricky to understand—it has much to do with sex and love, but a romantic nature (or the lack of one) surfaces in lots of ways, including how you interact with friends and strangers, as well as how calm or turbulent you are within yourself. Need some definitions? Well, the romantic wants to embellish reality, to make it more delightful, exciting, and wondrous than it actually is. The opposite of a romantic isn't a *cynic* (who is also given to imaginative embroidery, though of a negative kind), but the realist: she sees what *is*, and does not fluff up reality with her emotions or other frills.

This quiz is designed to detect whether or not you take the romantic view of life—and particularly of men—or a more cool-headed, realistic one. Since neither way of being is "better" than the other—any more than a poet is "superior" to a physicist—there's no reason to cheat. So be honest and *really* find out . . .

1. Which of the following best describes your belief about love?
a. The right man and the right woman can get through anything together.
b. Love is the *sine qua non* of life—I'd die without it!
c. It's important, but life offers many kinds of pleasure, and I'd never live for love alone.
d. True man-woman passion is so rare only a lucky few ever achieve it.

2. You would describe your women friends as:
a. Absolutely irreplaceable . . . our rapport is profound.
b. A valuable part of my life.
c. A little shallow . . . I wish my relationships with women had more depth.
d. Pleasant companions, but I live as I please, not as friends dictate.

3. Your latest bed partner would be likely to describe you as:
a. A caring, unselfish lover.
b. Brooding but passionate.
c. Physically very responsive, but in some way difficult to *reach*.
d. Sometimes stormy, sometimes gay . . . never, ever predictable!

4. You'd prefer an admirer who brought you:
a. Long-stemmed roses.
b. Wild flowers he picked himself.
c. Orchids.
d. A lovely flowering plant in full blossom.

5. When troubled by a black mood, you tend to:
a. Take to your bed for a few days if you can.
b. Try to block it out by undertaking some cheerful activity . . . seeing a good friend or an entertaining movie.
c. Become snappish, even, perhaps, a touch sardonic.
d. Lose yourself by *working* like a dervish!

6. You're attending a large party where most of the other guests are strangers. You're likely to feel:
a. Excited, parties are so full of possibilities.
b. Frustrated . . . it's so hard to make *contact* in a crowd.
c. Exhilarated for a while, but you tend to leave early, often in the company of an intriguing new man.
d. Somewhat bored . . . you prefer small, intimate gatherings.

7. Your favorite outfit is most likely:
a. Mauve or lavender   d. Bright red
b. Pale blue
c. Beige, brown, or black

8. When between serious affairs, you:
a. Say yes to most attractive males who come your way, but don't spend time with men who don't appeal physically.
b. Refuse invitations unless you think a man may be *the* one.
c. Go out constantly . . . friends wonder how you turn up such a stream of men.
d. Accept or decline invitations depending on how you feel that night.

9. Which of the following movie stars, based on her typical onscreen personality, best reflects your style?
a. Faye Dunaway   c. Liv Ullmann
b. Susan Sarandon   d. Sissy Spacek

10. You think the best marriages:
a. Happen when people are most temperamentally compatible.
b. Begin with passionate love then mellow into something beautiful and lasting.
c. Are sustained by really strong physical attraction.
d. Reflect powerful spiritual harmonies.

11. You think astrology is:
a. Amusing nonsense.
b. Irrational, but right often as not.
c. Uncannily true—though it's difficult to explain, the stars *do* oversee people's destinies.
d. An invaluable guide—you envy monarchs of old who had their own personal astrologers.

12. Which of the following would be true of you?
a. You've kept a journal of secret thoughts off and on since childhood.
b. You've never kept a journal.

c. You write voluminous notes to your self during times of crisis, but otherwise lack patience to keep a journal.

d. You've begun a journal at significant points in your life (just after entering college, starting a new job, falling in love), but never kept it up.

13. You believe jealousy is:

a. Wasted emotional energy . . . no one should compete for a loved one's attentions.

b. Inevitable when two people are passionately in love.

c. A sign love has begun to slip away.

d. Difficult and painful, but often unavoidable.

14. When wondering whether or not to get serious with a man, you'd consider a poor "past record" (an army of abandoned girl-friends, for instance) to be:

a. A turn-off—even if you try, you can't love a man with a nasty character.

b. A dead issue—what counts is what *you* have together.

c. Unnerving, but if you're strongly attracted, you persevere anyway!

d. Probably an indication that he hasn't yet met a woman sensitive enough to meet his needs.

15. The last few important men in your life were:

a. Very alike—they even looked a bit like each other.

b. Vividly different . . . what's the point of re-peating yourself in love?

c. All lovely, intelligent men . . . you wouldn't have been involved with them otherwise.

d. Similar in basic ways (the same character traits appeal to you), but different in looks and style.

16. Your mood cycles are:

a. Often unpredictable, sometimes you're gay when you ought to feel sad and vice versa.

b. Frequently linked to the weather and sea-sons . . . autumn makes you nostalgic, a rainy day stirs reveries.

c. A response to the actual events in your life.

d. Generally tethered to your situation, but sometimes a bleak or joyful mood seems to come from nowhere.

17. You believe sexual compatibility:

a. Always comes out of emotional harmony.

b. Reflects matching erotic tastes.

c. Follows mysterious laws of its own, and can be found between two people who have vir-tually nothing else in common.

d. Involves all of the above points.

18. You have chosen unsuitable loves (men who were very married, neurotic, impover-ished, or otherwise unattainable):

a. Often

b. Never

c. Sometimes

d. Only when an irresistible force *drew* you to-gether.

19. You believe a high level of sexual arousal with a new partner is:

a. The best indicator there is as to whether or not you'll become deeply involved.

b. A powerful magnet, but you'll give a man who doesn't spark all of those electrifying fire-showers a second or third chance.

c. An indication that you two wanted each other then, but not necessarily a forecast of love or even continued great sex.

d. A reflection of wondrously profound inner harmonies.

20. For your animal totem you would choose:
a. A black swan   c. A tigress
b. A doe   d. A racing filly

21. People often comment that your conversational style is:
a. Highly dramatic—you tell anecdotes and stories with great flair.
b. Brightest when you're talking about somebody else's adventures.
c. Dreamy and remote . . . you tend to wander from the point sometimes.
d. Reticent . . . you're more a listener than a talker.

SCORING: Give yourself points as follows.

1.	a.2	b.4	c.1	d.3	**12.**	a.3	b.1	c.4	d.2
2.	a.4	b.2	c.3	d.1	**13.**	a.1	b.4	c.3	d.2
3.	a.1	b.4	c.3	d.2	**14.**	a.1	b.4	c.2	d.3
4.	a.2	b.3	c.4	d.1	**15.**	a.3	b.4	c.1	d.2
5.	a.3	b.2	c.4	d.1	**16.**	a.4	b.3	c.1	d.2
6.	a.4	b.3	c.2	d.1	**17.**	a.3	b.1	c.4	d.2
7.	a.3	b.2	c.1	d.4	**18.**	a.4	b.1	c.2	d.3
8.	a.2	b.3	c.4	d.1	**19.**	a.4	b.2	c.1	d.3
9.	a.3	b.4	c.2	d.1	**20.**	a.3	b.2	c.4	d.1
10.	a.1	b.2	c.4	d.3	**21.**	a.4	b.2	c.3	d.1
11.	a.1	b.2	c.4	d.3					

Count up the number of 4, 3, 2, and 1 answers you gave. If you chose a majority of 4s, find your romance quotient under the heading Super Romantic. Mostly 3 answers means you're a Dreamy Romantic. A preponderance of 2s puts you in the company of Reasonable Romantics, and mostly 1s indicates you're a Realist. For a description of your type, see categories below.

The Super Romantic: You are stormily romantic, a lover of men and intrigue who'll abandon all in pursuit of passion. Lusty emotions rule you, and you always give first priority to affairs of the heart. Probably you've had several grand amours in your life, and look forward to many more! It's difficult for just one man to satisfy your heightened cravings for romance, and, for you, a settled, domestic love is pure tedium. If married, you'll probably look for excitement in affairs, but, truly, you're happiest at large—free to indulge even your most wayward impulse. Lucky you were born in our time, when a woman is as free to pursue passion as she is to study law. In another, more conservative era, you would have caused scandal, uproar, and at least two or three duels to the death!

The Dreamy Romantic: You, too, are a wild-eyed girl, but your style is very different from that of the sensation-hungry Super Romantic. Actually, you and she are equally hooked on romance, but in very different ways. She is a lusty individual while you are far more of a dreamer, losing yourself in reveries about the perfect man, and often wondering—sadly!—if you'll ever find him. Your deepest wish: a man you can love with absolutely no reservations, and you'll not settle for less. You want always to trust your mate, never to lie or be lied to, and live with him in unflawed harmony. In other centuries, girls like you usually gave up trying to find their ideal, and either signed into convents or stayed home to nurse Mother! In 1976, though, you'll probably keep looking for a prince and *not* find him. Yes, you may marry, even several times, but you soon grow disenchanted with anything less than the perfect mate. Take consolation in the richness of your inner life—it should help compensate for the annoying *human*ness of men.

The Reasonable Romantic: You indulge sometimes in hungry longings and sweet nostalgia, but you're not apt to let passions get totally out of control. You're too basically sane not to take joy in the world as it is, though you're romantic enough to view portions of it (including men you find particularly engaging) through a mauve-tinted glass. Fortunately, when you see a man as somewhat more desirable (richer, smarter, sweeter) than he actually is, often he responds to your loving interest by developing the very qualities with which you credit him. Your practical sense balances romantic leanings, and though you cry copiously over love stories or leave-takings, when the dramatic moment is over, you blot your eyes dry and remember the laundry needs doing.

The Realist: You call it as you see it, and you view life as astutely and precisely as anyone. Gauzy romance never filters your vision. Probably, you have never "fallen in love" in the romantic sense of the phrase, though you may have *loved* more deeply and truly than girls with more theatrical emotions. Because you view men—and everything else—with such good sense and accuracy, your decision to love is based on reality, not illusion, and is quite likely to last. Friends may think you somewhat prosaic, and even be irked by what seems to them an invulnerable nature. In truth, you are vulnerable—it's simply that you're moved by reality rather than fantasy. You are the stable one who's never deceived by men, but your love, once given, is intense, lasting, and true.

Are You Happy?

ROBERT HARRINGTON

Happiness is, alas, a fairly elusive quality. Most of us know when we're *un*happy, and we're often aware of *fleeting* joyous moments, but the question posed by this quiz—*how* happy are you?—can be a difficult one to answer. So let us do it for you! Read the responses to each question, then choose the one closest to your own feeling or situation. (And don't attempt to pick those that seem "happiest"—they aren't necessarily what they appear.) If none of the responses seems quite right, you may check *two* (but no more than two) or skip the question entirely. Do *try* to answer everything, though—*honestly!*

1. If given your pick of the following jobs, which would you choose?
a. A position in a very glamorous field where you'd meet many celebrities
b. A difficult, challenging assignment. If you can bring this off, you'll be promoted to an executive job.
c. A job you can excel in because it's ideally suited to your energies and talents
d. A fairly modest job which involves working closely with a powerful, important person

2. Do you enjoy doing favors?
a. Yes, I love helping out and I seldom refuse when asked.
b. Not really. But I do oblige when I feel I owe it to the person or if there's some compelling reason.

c. Yes, when it's not inconvenient and will really *help* someone.
d. I like doing favors for good friends or people important to me, but not the general public.

3. You've just met a man you find extremely attractive, and who seems to be attracted to *you*. What will you do?
a. Nothing specific—just let the situation develop and see what happens.
b. Talk to everyone who knows him and try to find out what sort of person he is.

c. Try to latch onto him—terrific men don't turn up every day!

d. Make sure he gets the message that I like him, then wait for *him* to make a move.

4. Which of these descriptions best fits your usual sleeping pattern?

a. Light sleeper, easily awakened

b. Sound sleeper, difficult to wake

c. Sound sleeper, but awakens easily when called

d. Sleeps lightly in beginning, more soundly toward morning

e. Sound sleep in beginning, more wakeful toward morning

5. Are there occasions when you feel a need to be completely alone, with no interruptions for a time?

a. Absolutely. Some of my most peaceful, creative moments come when I'm by myself.

b. No. I'm sociable and love having people around.

c. No. I don't mind being alone, but wouldn't say I have a need for it.

d. When the people around me are tiresome or obnoxious, yes. If they're interesting and amusing, no.

6. How important do you feel it is to keep your home, and office neat and orderly?

a. Very important. I can put up with sloppiness in others, but never in myself.

b. Unimportant. I'd rather be in a messy house where the people are relaxed than a tidy one where everybody's fussy and uptight.

c. Fairly important. I'm rather neat and don't much care for mess or squalor.

d. Important. In fact, I wish I were more orderly than I am.

7. Which of the following would you be *least* likely to want for a friend, lover, or acquaintance? The person who is . . . ?

a. Snobbish, pretentious, an inveterate name-dropper

b. Crude, pushy, ill-mannered

c. A bully, cruel to those who can't fight back

d. Grasping, selfish, miserly

8. In the last six months, how many times have you stayed home (for one day or many) because of illness?

a. None

b. One

c. Two or three

d. Four or more

9. During the past three years, how many times have you been hospitalized (for anything except childbirth)?

a. None

b. One

c. Two

d. Three or more

10. Unaccountably, you are offered a fabulous job as the star of a new Broadway musical, vice president in charge of publicity at a huge company, or the replacement for a recently resigned senator—something you'd love doing but for which you have virtually *no* qualifications. You would . . .

a. Accept. Whether I can handle the work or not, it's an opportunity that will never be repeated.

b. Refuse. Why disrupt my life for something I'd be no good at?

c. Accept if I thought I had even a small chance of succeeding, otherwise refuse.

d. Make it clear how unqualified I am. If they still want me, I'll accept.

11. Something distressing has happened to your man—the sudden death of someone close, perhaps, or the collapse of a project he's worked on for years. He's terribly upset. *Your* reaction?

a. I'd try everything possible to console him and cheer him up.

b. I'd be as upset as he was! When he hurts, I hurt, too.

c. Though sympathetic, I would leave him alone for a while. People in grief don't need others butting in.

d. I'd let him know I am sorry for his trouble, but would continue to treat him the way I normally do.

12. Do you usually arrive on time to work, appointments, dates? How punctual are you, really?

a. Extremely. I have a rather exact sense of time and am seldom late.

b. Quite *un*punctual, I'm afraid—even with an early start, I never seem to get anywhere on time.

c. I try to arrive when I'm supposed to, and usually succeed.

d. It varies. I'm punctual for some things, late for others.

13. You're about to leave on a trip abroad when you hear that a country you particularly wanted to visit is going through a period of riots, revolution, or terrorism and might be dangerous. Would you avoid that country?

a. Of course not, it sounds exciting!

b. I'd worry a little, but would probably go anyway.

c. I'd check with airlines, the State Department, the newspapers, and go if they said it was safe.

d. Who needs trouble on a vacation? I'd skip that country.

14. For how long do you remain angry with someone who has cheated or insulted you, been unfair or cruel?

a. A good long time. I don't easily forget or forgive bad treatment.

b. I wouldn't *get* angry. That sort of behavior is the product of a sick, troubled mind, and I'd be apt to feel pity for the person.

c. Not long. I get angry, but seldom hold a grudge.

d. I don't stay angry, but will usually avoid the person from then on.

15. A long-forgotten relative dies and leaves you a huge sum of money—several million dollars. How would you react to this windfall?

a. I'd be delighted!

b. There would be problems, of course—some people would be jealous and others would want loans or handouts—but send the money anyway!

c. I'd rather earn than be given my millions—that's my only reservation.

d. I'd be quite worried about handling such a huge sum—it would mean starting a whole new life.

16. From the following list, check the three qualities you would find most appealing in a man. Should he be . . . ?

a. Extremely good-looking

b. Rich and powerful

c. Intelligent, well-educated

d. Compatible, sharing your interests and goals

e. Celebrated and glamorous

f. Sexy, a terrific lover   **g.** Amusing and witty

h. Kind, gentle, understanding
i. Sensitive, artistic, talented
j. Strong, supercompetent, a leader

17. What are your feelings about death?

a. It terrifies me; I try not to think about it.
b. Death is just a natural part of the life cycle. I'll probably accept it when the time comes.
c. It seems remote, especially since medical science keeps adding more years to our lives.
d. There's so much I want to do. I'd hate it if death interrupted me too soon.
e. I know we could all die at any moment, but the subject doesn't seem very important to me just now.

18. Are you gregarious, or not? Which of the following statements best describes your social style?

a. I'm highly selective and tend to keep to a small circle of good, close friends.
b. I'm very active socially and know literally hundreds of people.
c. I have a lot of friends but don't stay in touch with them. I usually associate with whomever is nearby or comes to see me.
d. My friends are a large, congenial group who know each other well and see each other often.

19. Many people have a highly subjective sense of time. Do you? With which of these statements would you agree?

a. Time generally passes quickly, almost in a blur.
b. It seems to move rather slowly.
c. Days are long, but weeks and months really speed by.
d. Days seem fast, weeks and months slow.

e. None of the above. My time sense is quite normal.

20. This may seem an awfully large question, but how do you feel right now about your entire situation—personal assets and qualities, friends and lovers, life style, career, prospects for the future?

a. Wonderful! Things are going extremely well, and the future looks beautiful, too!
b. Pretty good. My situation may not be marvelous, but it's okay, and improving steadily.
c. Good, I'd say, but that's not enough for me. I'm striving for a *much* better future!
d. My feelings vary. Sometimes I feel good about myself, sometimes not. Can't really answer the question.

ANSWER SECTION: What does it *mean* to be happy? Well, the great students of human nature—whether poets or philosophers, doctors of theology or doctors of medicine—have always agreed that happiness *isn't* a separate state or condition which can occur by itself. Instead, it's a *by-product,* an emotion we feel when things are going well, when we're living well, being useful and productive. The happy person is also what the psychologist calls "well-adjusted."

Are *you* happy? Let's see. Check your answers against our list. Only the "happy" answer to each question counts. If you check that one, give yourself a point; otherwise, nothing.

ANSWERS 1.d, 2.c, 3.a, 4.c, 5.c, 6.c, 7.c, 8.a or b, 9.a or b, 10.c, 11.d, 12.c, 13.b, 14.c, 15.a, 16.d, 17.e, 18.c, 19.d, 20.b

SCORING: If you got 3 points or less, there isn't, unfortunately, much joy in your life. Five is better and 7 very good—you experience many happy moments. To qualify as a happy *person*, though, you'll need 9 to 12 points. (A score much higher than that would be rather amazing.)

Don't be too disappointed if your results show you're less than totally happy, though. Great happiness can actually be a handicap in many respects. Because happy people tend not to be greedy, it's hard for them to become extremely rich. What's more, being deficient in hard-driving ambition, they don't often ascend to powerful positions. And since they refuse to be rigidly perfectionistic, they seldom turn out great works of art.

This quiz was based on a number of traits that have been found to be common among happy, well-adjusted people. Following is a description of each trait, along with the number of numbers of the questions where "right" answers suggest you possess these happy qualities.

The happy person likes to do useful, productive work, to use her abilities fully (1, 10, 12). She enjoys helping people, but is not self-sacrificing (2). She's confident and easygoing, rather than overeager or anxious, about sex (3). At night, sleep researchers have found, she usually falls into a deep, sometimes dreamless sleep, from which she awakes easily and abruptly (4). She tends to be self-sufficient and can enjoy both solitude and company but is dependent on neither (5, 18). Generally, she's orderly and punctual (6, 12). Though tolerant of people's minor flaws, she dislikes cruelty, unfairness, and destructiveness (7). She is healthy (8, 9), has no hang-ups about success or prosperity (10, 15), and refuses to participate in other people's negative emotions (11)—*or* cling to her own (14). She's confident in high-risk situations (13) and un-fearful about death (13, 17). When choosing a mate, she will pick a congenial, compatible figure rather than someone romantic and glamorous (16). Like many busy, absorbed people, she feels her days pass quickly, though in larger units—weeks, months, years—time may seem endless (19). The reverse is true for bored folk: Their days drag on slowly, but the months flit by. Finally, the happy person has a sense of progress, improvement, of getting somewhere (20). Without this, she would cease to be happy.

Are You a Giver, Or a Taker?

JUNIUS ADAMS

Are you open-handedly, open-heartedly generous, or do you frankly, with no apologies, give top priority to your own interests? Also, which is it *better* to be—a totally selfless giver or an enlightened taker? Our quiz will answer both these questions, but first you must respond—*honestly*—to each hypothetical situation with the statement that most closely fits your own opinions and desires.

1. A sorcerer tells you he is about to transform you into one of the following women and make you relive her life. You can't escape, but are offered a choice. Whom would you rather be?
a. A world-famous political influence—Eleanor Roosevelt or Mme. Chiang Kai-Shek
b. A romantic poet—Edna St. Vincent Millay or Elizabeth Barrett Browning
c. The heiress to a great fortune—Dina Merrill
d. A renowned and talented beauty—Elizabeth Taylor

2. In a store, you'd be *most* apt to buy an item if it were . . .
a. Of exceptional quality, built to last and bring pleasure for many years
b. A fabulous bargain, selling well under the regular price
c. Unusually beautiful, of superb design
d. Something new and clever that would amuse or amaze your friends

3. A man has the best chance of attracting you if he is . . .
a. Rich, powerful, or famous
b. Infatuated, finds *you* irresistible
c. Sexy, friendly, a good match
d. Someone you can be important to and help to achieve his full potential

4. A good friend has suffered some great misfortune—gone bankrupt or lost her husband. You would . . .

a. Feel sorry, of course, but also a little annoyed. You can't help believing that people often bring their troubles on themselves.
b. Do everything you could to help her recover from the setback.
c. Be sorry for her and also for yourself—she's been terribly depressed lately, and her friendship is no longer as enjoyable as it once was.
d. Feel concerned and try to find ways to cheer her up.

5. You've been invited to spend the weekend at someone's country house and have just embarked on a strict, all-protein diet. What will you do?

a. Explain your diet beforehand so they won't be surprised.
b. Bring along a lot of steaks to make things easy for the hostess.
c. Decide to make do with lots of eggs and cottage cheese or whatever is in their fridge.
d. Abandon the diet over the weekend—you'll start again Monday.

6. You're campaigning for political office and have uncovered information that, if known, would damage your opponent's reputation and chances. Your next move would be to . . .

a. Call a press conference and release the information—that's what he'd do in your place!
b. Hold the information and use it only if that seems your only chance of winning.
c. Disclose the facts if you feel doing so is your duty; otherwise, keep quiet.

d. Refuse to use the information under any circumstances. You will *not* smear someone in order to win.

7. Your man has bought you a piece of jewelry which, though expensive, *isn't* something you would have wanted or chosen for yourself. Your reaction is to . . .

a. Feel pleased and impressed by the extravagance of the purchase.
b. Ask him to exchange the piece for something that really suits you.
c. Feel flattered by the gesture, but also a bit upset at his having wasted his money.
d. Return the jewelry yourself and exchange it for several less expensive baubles you really like.

8. Of *course* you love your job! You would, however, quit in a minute if . . .

a. You no longer felt needed there.
b. You were asked to take on tasks you found demeaning or insulting.
c. You realized your job was a dead end, with no further opportunities for advancement.
d. The work became much more complicated or difficult.

9. Let's say you're a doctor or a lawyer. Will you give free medical or legal advice to your friends if asked?

a. Certainly—a friend is a friend!
b. Probably, as long as they don't make complete nuisances of themselves.
c. Only with very casual questions, or in a real emergency.
d. No! People are more apt to remain friends if they don't take advantage of each other.

10. At a gambling casino, a male companion gives you a handful of chips to bet on some

game you're unfamiliar with. You would probably . . .

a. Bet the chips at random, hoping for luck.
b. Observe the play for a while and try to figure out how the game works, *then* bet.
c. Ask him to bet for you or tell you what to play.
d. Place a few bets and see how your luck is running. If you win, fine; if not, you can always cash in whatever chips are left.

11. A friend has tried to cheat you—she made a purchase for you and is withholding most of the change. You would . . .

a. Be quite angered and outraged, and tell her so.
b. Insist on getting the money back, and be more wary in dealing with her from now on.
c. Feel sorry that she finds it necessary to stoop to petty swindles, but let her get away with her ploy.
d. Say nothing, but begin to see her less frequently.

12. Your man has asked you to spend the weekend with him at a marvelous resort you've been itching to visit. At the last moment, however, he cancels the trip because of some important business. You'd no doubt . . .

a. Be quite disappointed, and forgive him only if he promises to reschedule the trip *soon*.
b. Assure him you understand and say you don't mind, even if you *do*.
c. Let him know how disappointed you are without making an issue of it.
d. Feel sorry for *both* of you.

13. You've just bought a lovely silk blouse that was supposedly on sale, only to discover the same item selling for much less at another shop just around the corner. You . . .

a. Feel relatively unconcerned. Why worry about a few dollars when so many problems in life are more important?
b. Feel cheated and resolve not to shop anymore at the store where you bought the blouse.
c. Return the blouse for a refund and buy another at the less expensive shop.
d. Warn your friends not to fall for the phony "sale."

14. You don't often drop a friend, but would be most apt to if she had . . .

a. Insulted you rather badly with no provocation
b. Turned into a whining complainer
c. Been cruel to someone else you know
d. Become snooty and pretentious in the aftermath of some real or fancied success in life

15. With which of these rather sweeping statements would you be most apt to agree? Life is . . .

a. A struggle in which each of us stands alone and must remain vigilant in order to survive.
b. A foreordained process in most cases. Since we can't change its course very much, we may as well learn to enjoy whatever happens.
c. An endless series of challenges which bring success or failure, depending on how we meet them.
d. A process in which the more we contribute, the more we ultimately get back.

SCORING: Circle each of your answers in the following table:

1.	a.P b.O c.M d.N	9.	a.P b.O c.N d.M
2.	a.N b.M c.O d.P	10.	a.P b.N c.O d.M
3.	a.M b.N c.O d.P	11.	a.O b.M c.P d.N
4.	a.N b.P c.M d.O	12.	a.M b.O c.N d.P
5.	a.M b.N c.O d.P	13.	a.O b.N c.M d.P
6.	a.M b.N c.O d.P	14.	a.N b.M c.P d.O
7.	a.O b.M c.P d.N	15.	a.M b.O c.N d.P
8.	a.P b.O c.N d.M		

Count the number of *M*s, *N*s, *O*s, and *P*s you scored. The letter most often circled represents your dominant mode of giving or taking.

M: Ruthlessness. Determinedly self-assertive, you go wholeheartedly after what you want, and too bad for those who get in your way. You believe in playing to win, and are mildly contemptuous of anyone who doesn't. And often you *do* win, single-minded as you are in the pursuit of your goals. Just beware of appearing grumpy, grudging, or insensitive. Remember, you *do* need people, and should be careful not to alienate them unnecessarily. The world despises a "taker" who appears boorish but adores one who can exhibit grace, charm, and wit—someone like the late John F. Kennedy, for instance.

N: Enlightened Self-Interest. A majority of *N*s denotes someone who is confident and outgoing, able to express her desires easily and pursue them without pushiness or ferocity. You don't mind helping others on occasion, but feel that to be truly useful to those you love, your own needs must first be satisfied. As a competitor, you're effective but relaxed—unperturbed when once in a while you must yield to a more anxious or insistent opponent. Normally friendly and equable, you can nonetheless become a tigress when anyone tries to cheat, trick, or demean you.

O: Humanitarianism. Because you're so rich yourself—in inner strength and self-regard, if not material wealth—you're able to give more than other people. You undoubtedly have many friends who are attracted to you because of your warmth, generosity, and quiet self-confidence, and you enjoy becoming involved in their problems and aspirations. While helping gives you great satisfaction, however, you're no patsy—those who attempt to use or abuse your good nature for selfish ends are quickly rebuffed.

P: Selflessness. Other people come first in your scheme of things, and much of your life is devoted to pleasing them. You'll run errands for friends, help with their chores, nurse them when they're sick, lend them money when they need it, and listen attentively to their woes even when your own are more acute or pressing. While you can be a marvelous companion and confidante, however, people would like you even better if you weren't quite so *diligent* in attending to them. Try to be selfish at least *some* of the time!

Which type—giver or taker—*should* you be? Well, both have obvious merits, but you'll be happier and more successful if your score shows six or eight "taking" answers—givers are often unable to fight hard enough for what they want and need. The best score is one in which no more than seven answers are in any one of the four categories, with the remainder distributed fairly evenly throughout the other three.

How Mature Are You?

ERNEST DICHTER, PH.D.

Have you ever worried that you're still a *child* so far as feelings are concerned? Each of the following questions has three possible answers. Check the one that seems most descriptive of your emotional reactions. Be honest! You want to find out how old you *really* are, don't you?

1. A man crying in public or on a TV news program attracts your attention. Your immediate reaction:
a. You're slightly embarrassed and feel like turning away.
b. You feel sympathetic although you think he should really have more self-control.
c. You think, if women are allowed to cry, why not men, too?

2. You hear about the sudden death in an accident of two of your friends.
a. You are very upset, and call various people who knew them to discuss the tragedy.
b. You become depressed for days—such a useless end to two people's lives!
c. Though saddened, you reflect that tragedy can strike anyone, even yourself, and you try to put the incident out of your mind.

3. Seeing a mother cover herself with mud at the beach and prance around giggling hysterically in front of her children, you think:
a. Sometimes it's good to be a child again.
b. A grown-up ought to be a little more dignified.

c. It's O.K. to make children laugh, but she should use a less ridiculous method.

4. Your husband or boyfriend forgets your birthday or wedding anniversary. You would:

a. Not say a word, so as not to embarrass him.

b. Use various subtle approaches to make him remember.

c. Become quite upset and show your annoyance in little refusals and various forms of retaliation.

5. An aunt of yours develops a probably incurable cancer. Which one of these attitudes do you think she should take about her situation?

a. Resign herself to the inevitable and put her affairs in order.

b. Carry on her normal life as if nothing had happened.

c. Go on a trip around the world and see all her favorite countries before she dies.

6. The year has been terrible for you. All sorts of things didn't work out: You met only boring or hateful men, lost money in a business venture and failed to get a promotion at the office. Your reaction:

a. You feel you've had poor luck, perhaps as a result of bad karma.

b. To break the pattern, you buy new clothes and splurge on a good vacation.

c. You don't worry much because you know that two months from now you will have forgotten all those setbacks, for your luck will have changed.

7. Looking back, you see that you made a wrong decision. If you hadn't yelled at your man, you could have avoided a bad quarrel, or if you had taken the new job offer, you would have been happier and more prosperous. You feel:

a. Somewhat regretful and upset at your lack of judgment.

b. Unconcerned because an opportunity to do better is bound to arrive soon.

c. Eager to figure out how to correct your error.

8. You win a large amount of money in a lottery. You would:

a. Celebrate and buy several things you've always wanted but couldn't afford.

b. Spend very little at first while gradually deciding how to change your life.

c. Buy only the *most* important things and put the rest of the money aside for the future.

9. The papers carry news of muggings, rape, corruption. Your reaction is to:

a. Think about moving to another locality where things are more pleasant.

b. Join a group that is trying to clean up your neighborhood or set up anti-crime patrols.

c. Join an organization that is working to publicize the bad conditions and pressure the authorities into improving them.

10. What do you think of this statement: The most satisfying philosophy is to enjoy life and try to get the most out of it.

a. Very realistic and practical, although some hypocrites would disagree.

b. A selfish and shortsighted attitude.

c. Wrong: One has to mix pleasure and duty in a *proper* fashion.

11. Your life so far has been fairly successful. You would ascribe your success mainly to:

a. Hard work and real motivation to achieve your goals.

b. Luck, to a large extent—you didn't really

do all *that* much to earn your good fortune.

c. Knowing what you wanted through good instincts, a little luck.

12. In a real emergency, would most of the people you know turn to you for help?
a. Yes, because you're resourceful and practical.
b. No, because they'll be looking for a strong leader, which you are not.
c. Yes, because they'll need someone sympathetic who can understand problems, as you think you can.

13. Adding up the happy and unhappy moments in your life up to now, what percentages would you pick:
a. Happy moments 50%; Unhappy moments 50%.
b. Happy moments 30%; Unhappy moments 70%.
c. Happy moments 70%; Unhappy moments 30%.

SCORING TABLE:

1.	a.1	b.2	c.3		**8.**	a.1	b.2	c.3
2.	a.2	b.1	c.3		**9.**	a.1	b.3	c.2
3.	a.3	b.1	c.2		**10.**	a.1	b.2	c.3
4.	a.3	b.2	c.1		**11.**	a.2	b.1	c.3
5.	a.2	b.3	c.1		**12.**	a.1	b.2	c.3
6.	a.2	b.1	c.3		**13.**	a.3	b.1	c.2
7.	a.1	b.2	c.3					

ANALYSIS OF ANSWERS

29 to 39 points: *Highly mature.* Whatever your actual age, you are a full-fledged *adult*. Emotional maturity as I see it is not a matter of cold, rational behavior, but of accepting reality and fun as a part of life, being happy with oneself, and remaining open to further growth and development. Answers which show this attitude, for instance, are 1 (c) accepting emotionality; 3 (a) tolerating uninhibited behavior; or 8 (c) being restrained but not overly so in your expenditures.

20 to 28 points: *"Overly" mature.* You tend to be a little stiff, restrained or cautious in your attitudes, which could actually make you seem *older* than you are. Loosen up a little, and you'll have more fun! Typical of the over-mature attitude are answers like 1 (b) low tolerance for public display of emotions; 7 (a) not being able to forget past mistakes; or 11 (a) over-insistence on the work ethic.

13 to 19 points: *Somewhat mature.* Probably you have considerable charm and are often amusing to be with but—admit it!—you can be downright *childish* at times. Answers which show this trait are 6 (b) or 8 (a) self-indulgence; 9 (a) avoiding unpleasant realities; or 13 (b) over-gloominess. You should try to accept more responsibility for your life and actions and also learn to curb your often over-exuberant or unrealistic emotions.

How Suspicious Are You?

LOUISE MORGAN

Are you a trusting girl, sauntering ingenuously through life, depending unconditionally upon other people's kindness? A cynic who believes in *maybe* trusting blood, but surely going no further than that? Or somewhere in the middle, assessing people and situations as they come along, hoping for the good, but also prepared to deal with disappointment? Take this test to find out, and do be honest—false answers simply cheat *you* of invaluable insight.

SECTION I—Mark each statement True or False.

1. My friends adorn my life—they are stylish, self-controlled, and unusually accomplished. ____

2. I have sometimes allowed a man into my bed after only a date or two. ____

3. Other people often trust me with their secrets. ____

4. I have a warm, relaxed relationship with my mother. ____

5. People seldom lie to me. ____

6. I enjoy huge parties where I know only a few of the guests. ____

7. The balance of my savings is generally several times larger than what I keep in my checking account. ____

8. I sometimes pick up hitchhikers if they seem harmless. ____

9. I seldom make personal friends in the office. ____

10. In a crisis, I seek advice from one or several confidantes. ____

11. I loathe blind dates. ____

12. At least two of the men in my life have been absolute rotters. ____

13. I never give money to panhandlers. ____

14. I enjoy chatting with taxi drivers and other amiable strangers. ____

15. Friends consider me self-reliant. ____

SECTION II—Complete the following statements by supplying the word or words that seem *most* appropriate to you.

1. Girls who fall in love every few weeks are ____
a. Impetuous
b. Indiscriminate
c. Passionate

2. ____ **people value self-interest over co-operation.**
a. A few
b. All
c. The majority of

3. People with ____ **usually get ahead fastest.**
a. Boldness
b. Talent
c. Dedication

4. Men usually jilt women because they are ____.
a. Attracted to someone else
b. Tired of being watchdogged
c. Cads who can't sustain long relationships

5. The man who'd permit a woman to support him could best be described as ____.
a. Passive
b. Exploitative
c. Liberated

6. Girls who marry ____ **have made a sound choice.**
a. "Up"
b. For love
c. The likeliest available candidate

7. Lovers who kiss and fondle in public are ____.
a. Passionately enamored
b. Probably faking
c. Highly exhibitionistic

8. Marriages based on ____ **are likely to last.**
a. Shared goals and purposes
b. Strong affection
c. Powerful sexual attraction

9. Men who rise to positions of leadership are ____.
a. Shrewd and able
b. Selflessly devoted
c. Fiercely ambitious

10. Any friendship not based on ____ **is sure to founder.**
a. Mutual self-interest
b. Honesty and respect
c. Lively affection

11. The woman who says she still has nightly sex with her husband of five years is _____.
a. Probably lying
b. Passionately in love
c. Libidinally overactive

12. Girls who have trouble connecting with men are _____.
a. Beset by ill luck
b. Neurotically selfish
c. Unrealistically romantic

SECTION III—Choose the answer that most nearly describes your reaction in the following situations.

1. You meet a very attractive stranger at a party. When he asks if he might see you again, you—
a. Make a date for the following Saturday night
b. Stall—then find out more about him from your hostess
c. Suggest a lunchtime meeting
d. Say you'd enjoy a quiet drink or two after the party ends

2. A co-worker is reputed to be treacherous and double-dealing. You—
a. Are sweet and solicitous around her—best to have this viper on your side
b. Disregard her reputation until you see evidence of shoddy conduct
c. Determine to fight if she crosses you
d. Keep your contacts with her as minimal as possible

3. You are in bed for the first time with a man who makes an enormous effort to please. You—
a. Reciprocate the favor—he deserves sensational loving in return.
b. Are made a little *shy* by his intensity; still, you're delighted by these loving attentions.
c. Think he's probably one of those Don Juans who offers a woman little else *except* artful love-making. Accomplished sexual technicians can be *trouble!*

4. You've begun to feel major stirrings for a particular man, but are not yet sure of his feelings for you. You—
a. Confess your fondness for him—you simply cannot disguise such powerful emotions
b. Subdue your feelings when he's around—the one who feels most deeply *always* loses leverage in a relationship
c. Cultivate other admirers so as to stop over-focusing on a man you cannot count upon
d. Go with the flow but say nothing about your feelings until relatively sure they're reciprocated

5. You have been charged with training an office subordinate and you find her unsympathetic, self-seeking, and untrustworthy. You—
a. Train her as completely as possible, since that's your job. You're not being paid to *like* the girl.
b. Give as little help as you can without endangering your own position.
c. Tell higher-ups you'd appreciate it if somebody else could be persuaded to supervise this girl's work.
d. Share only a small *part* of your expertise—should she become too accomplished, she'd try to get *your* job.

6. You generally—
a. Pay all bills at the beginning of the month after cursory scrutiny
b. Double-check all itemized statements to be sure they're correct.

7. A stranger rings your bell in the middle of the evening, saying he's a good friend of your brother's and has just arrived in town. You—
a. Keep the door bolted and ask a few questions to be sure he's the person he *says* he is
b. Invite him in
c. Explain you're busy just then, but suggest he drop by your office at lunchtime the following day

8. A man who's led you to believe you're the only woman in his life is, you accidentally discover, sleeping with two other girls. Your reaction is to—
a. Cashier the affair. If he's lied once, he'll lie again.
b. Confront him with your discovery and forgive him after a short but stormy quarrel.
c. Think it was probably just a tactful fib and let the matter go without making a fuss.
d. Tell him calmly that you know he lied and insist on greater honesty in the future.

9. A good friend repeatedly borrows smallish sums of money and neglects to repay them. You—
a. Think little about it. Probably she's just careless with cash.
b. Remind yourself of this friend's many *good* qualities—you enjoy her too much in other ways to fuss over a quite minor flaw.
c. Tell her the unpaid loans bother you and ask her to *please* pay you back in the future.
d. Consider packing the friendship in—if

she's willing to exploit you in little ways, she'll sell you out in the *big* things, too.

10. You've arrived alone at a secluded pond where you notice a group of tough-looking adolescent boys. You—
a. Promptly decide to save your swimming for another day.
b. Engage them in conversation. If they *sound* menacing, leave quickly, if not, enjoy your swim.
c. Disregard them and plunge.

11. A decent, likable, but *unexciting* man wants to take you on a glamorous island junket. He *understands* (he says!) that you don't want to sleep with him and merely craves the pleasure of your company. You—
a. Take him at his word and go.
b. Assume he's lying and, as you don't find him sexually attractive, decide to stay home.
c. Expect that his resolve, though honorable, will melt beneath tropical sunshine but go anyway. You feel you can "handle" him.

12. The following people have keys to your apartment—
a. The super, your boyfriend, your closest neighbor
b. Just the super
c. The super and your man-friend of the moment

SCORING: Give yourself points as follows—

SECTION I	SECTION II	SECTION III
1. T.1 F.5	**1.** a.3 b.1 c.5	**1.** a.3 b.2 c.1 d.4
2. T.5 F.1	**2.** a.5 b.1 c.3	**2.** a.3 b.4 c.1 d.2
3. T.5 F.1	**3.** a.1 b.5 c.3	**3.** a.4 b.2 c.1
4. T.5 F.1	**4.** a.1 b.3 c.5	**4.** a.4 b.3 c.1 d.2
5. T.1 F.5	**5.** a.3 b.1 c.5	**5.** a.4 b.2 c.1 d.3
6. T.5 F.1	**6.** a.1 b.5 c.3	**6.** a.4 b.1
7. T.1 F.5	**7.** a.5 b.1 c.3	**7.** a.1 b.4 c.2
8. T.5 F.1	**8.** a.1 b.3 c.5	**8.** a.1 b.3 c.4 d.2
9. T.1 F.5	**9.** a.3 b.5 c.1	**9.** a.4 b.3 c.2 d.1
10. T.5 F.1	**10.** a.1 b.3 c.5	**10.** a.1 b.3 c.4
11. T.1 F.5	**11.** a.1 b.5 c.3	**11.** a.4 b.1 c.3
12. T.5 F.1	**12.** a.5 b.1 c.3	**12.** a.4 b.1 c.3
13. T.1 F.5		
14. T.5 F.1		
15. T.1 F.5		

If you scored between 39 and 70 points, you are a *Super-Cynic.* Between 70 and 105 points means you are a *Healthy Skeptic. Trusting Girls* score from 105 to 140 points, and if your total was over 140, you are a *Gullible Babe.* See below for a profile of your type.

Super-Cynic: You are canny and strong-minded, a woman who must be *shown!* Gifted with formidable intelligence, your mind seeks *tirelessly* for weakness in those around you. You expect perfidy and meet evidence of treachery with something very like satisfaction. You *knew* your confidence wasn't merited and are almost pleased that misgiving—your near-constant companion—was justified once again. Since you're so well-armored against betrayal, you make friends slowly, never wholly giving up your trust. The price of such elaborate fortifications? Your suspicious nature isolates you, leads to a higher-than-average level of inner tension. Do try to loosen up. Therapy might help!

Healthy Skeptic: You are a smart, astute girl who casts a clear, unprejudiced eye over the world around you and sees people as they actually *are.* You have few friends—you're never really *anxious* to bestow your trust—but these few are true and tested and you place your entire confidence in them. In truth, you are not overly suspicious, merely prudent, watchful, and smart! With your clear, receptive mind, you expect neither too little nor too much from other people and put your faith only in those who truly *deserve*.

Trusting Girl: You expect the best from people and, because of your own optimistic buoyancy and gay good nature, you often get it! Indeed, you cannot understand those purveyors of doom who seem always to be *warning* you against this one or that one. Sometimes, though, you should pay attention to these worriers. Your shimmering expectations aren't *often* disappointed, but even your blessed life has contained some less-than-golden moments. Protect your emotions against unhappy jolts by keeping billowing hopes in *control!*

Gullible Babe: Dear girl, you really *might* have been born yesterday. You are childishly credulous, always thinking the shining best of people! And because it's so sinfully easy to take advantage of your lamblike nature, exploiters do crowd 'round, bruising your emotions and devastating that too freely given trust. Is there *help* for you? It would do little good to aspire to shrewdness—canny you will never be—but with diligent practice you could, and *should*, develop a healthy modicum of skepticism and reserve.

Your Magnificent Mind

It's not just what you *are* that counts in life, but also what you *know*. Informed women are more articulate and persuasive than ignorant bunnies because they have so much more to *say*. And while innate intelligence is hardly to be discounted, you can *enhance* the brains you were born with by boning up.

This part of the book measures your mental acumen. First, find out if potholes mar your education or if you're already an accomplished mistress of language, history, and the arts. Next, take our 25-Minute I.Q. test to see how quickly you make the right (clever!) connections. (If you're more educated than basically smart, congratulations are in order—see how far you've *come!*) Next find out how much you know about fancy foods and wines. (Sophisticated women *don't* ask French waiters for translations!) And a knowledge of trivia can be more important than it seems—command of the interesting odd tidbit makes your conversation more *piquante*.

The last two subjects covered here are vital to *survival*. You can't afford *not* to be savvy about finances in these super-inflationary times. And knowing your nutrition is the first step to fitness and health. Find out if your present diet is as good for you as it truly *should* be.

How Well Educated Are You?

ABBY ADAMS

Were you the kind of student who spent her most *passionate* hours in the library, who still loves to cuddle up beside an enchanting book? Or are you a semischolar? Take this quiz to judge your store of fascinating and useful knowledge—the kind you absorb in *and* out of school. If you flunk, no one will force you to repeat the course, though there's always time to learn—if you *want* to!

1. What is the philosophers' stone?
a. According to Greek mythology, it gave magical powers to its possessor.
b. An imaginary substance medieval alchemists believe would turn lead into gold.
c. A corner of the marketplace in Athens where Socrates lectured.
d. One of the crown jewels of England used in the coronation ceremony.

2. The towns in Charles Dickens's *A Tale of Two Cities* **are . . .**
a. London and Edinburgh.
b. London and New York.
c. London and Manchester.
d. London and Paris.

3. Match these eight foreign phrases with the following translations. You get two points extra credit if you also identify all languages correctly.
a. *Bel canto*
b. *A priori*
c. *Lebensraum*

1. Pet peeve
2. Living space
3. Secretly

d. *Chiaroscuro*
e. *Sub rosa*
f. *Weltschmerz*
g. *Bête noire*
h. *Fait accompli*

4. Light and shade (in painting)
5. Fine singing
6. A thing already done
7. World-weariness
8. Before the fact

4. What style of architecture is exemplified by the Parthenon?
a. Doric
b. Ionic
c. Corinthian
d. Romanesque

5. *Don Quixote* **by Cervantes is a . . .**
a. Parody.
b. Slander.
c. Travesty.
d. Satire.

6. Dinosaurs lived during the _____ age.
a. Paleozoic.
b. Pleistecene
c. Cenozoic
d. Mesozoic

7. Match the composer to the composition.
a. Verdi
b. Bach
c. Debussy
d. Beethoven
e. Stravinsky
f. Mozart

1. *Goldberg Variations*
2. *The Afternoon of a Faun*
3. *The Fire Bird*
4. *Falstaff*
5. *Fidelio*
6. *The Marriage of Figaro*

8. What does *ibid*. in a footnote mean?
a. Refers to another book by the same author
b. Indicates further reference to a source just cited
c. Indicates a misspelling or unorthodox usage
d. Refers to a previous page of the same book

9. Spontaneous generation is . . .
a. The discredited theory that living creatures can originate in nonliving matter.
b. A fire that begins with accumulated internal heat.
c. Asexual reproduction.
d. Revolutions exploding in different parts of the world at the same time.

10. Drury Lane is . . .
a. A mistress of King Charles II of England.
b. A story by Dickens.
c. An early Beatles song.
d. A theater in London.

11. Match these noted scientists to their achievements.
a. Sir Isaac Newton
b. Albert Einstein
c. Edward Jenner
d. Guglielmo Marconi
e. Marie Curie
f. Sir William Harvey

1. Discovered circulation of the blood
2. Invented the wireless telegraph
3. Discovered the element radium
4. Originated vaccination for smallpox
5. Author of the theory of relativity
6. Discovered the law of gravity

12. St. Francis of Assisi can be described as an . . .
a. Aesthete.
b. Ascetic.
c. Atheist.

13. In the problem $\frac{2}{3}x = 40$, what is x?
a. 60
b. 36
c. 20
d. 54

14. What's wrong with the following sentence? *Wandering through the forest, it suddenly began to rain.*
a. Mixed metaphor
b. Split infinitive
c. Ending with a preposition
d. Dangling participle

15. Match the names of these ancient Greeks with their callings:
a. Pericles
b. Sappho
c. Sophocles
d. Socrates
e. Praxiteles
f. Euclid

1. Poet
2. Sculptor
3. Playwright
4. Mathematician
5. Philosopher
6. Statesman

16. The philosophic belief that people must find their own purpose in a meaningless universe through exercising free will is known as . . .
a. Nihilism.
b. Determinism.
c. Existentialism.
d. Materialism.

17. What European country fits this description? *Once ruled by Rome, Spain, France, and Germany, it is now an independent constitutional monarchy.*
a. Italy
c. Portugal
b. Sweden
d. The Netherlands

18. Pierre, Natasha, André, and Sonia are characters in what Russian novel?
a. *Crime and Punishment* by Dostoevsky
b. *War and Peace* by Tolstoy
c. *The Cherry Orchard* by Chekhov
d. *Doctor Zhivago* by Pasternak

19. Arrange these historical events in chronological order, from one to ten:
a. The Norman conquest
b. The charge of the Light Brigade
c. The Trojan War
d. The Louisiana Purchase
e. The fall of the Roman Empire
f. The Children's Crusade
g. The Teapot Dome scandal
h. The defeat of the Spanish Armada
i. The Dreyfus affair
j. The Black Death

20. Which of the following plays was *not* written by Shakespeare?
a. Love's Labour's Lost
c. All For Love
b. Measure for Measure
d. As You Like It

21. What number comes next in this progression? 4, 5, 3, 6, 2, 7, 1, 8, 0 . . .
a. 9
c. 10
b. 4
d. 12

22. Match these poets with quotations from their works:
a. Samuel Coleridge
d. Alexander Pope
b. John Keats
e. T.S. Eliot
c. Emily Dickinson
f. William Blake

1. "My heart aches, and a drowsy numbness pains/My sense, as though of hemlock I had drunk."
2. "April is the cruellest month, breeding/Lilacs out of the dead land."
3. "Know then thyself, presume not God to scan/The proper study of mankind is man."
4. "Tyger! Tyger! burning bright/In the forests of the night./What immortal hand or eye/Could frame thy fearful symmetry."
5. "Hope is the thing with feathers/That perches in the soul."
6. "As idle as a painted ship/Upon a painted ocean."

23. What happened at Sarajevo?
a. In August 1914, Kaiser Wilhelm declared war on France and Russia.
b. In June 1914, Archduke Francis Ferdinand was assassinated.
c. In July 1914, Serbia declared its independence.
d. Marshal Tito was born in 1892.

24. The planet Pluto was discovered in . . .
a. 1949
c. 1914
b. 1930
d. 1892

25. Match the artist's name to the movement with which he is associated:
a. Matisse
1. Surrealism
b. Seurat
2. Abstract expressionism
c. Braque
3. Cubism
d. Monet
4. Fauvism
e. Magritte
5. Pointillism
f. Pollock
6. Impressionism

26. Madame de Maintenon was . . .
a. Mistress of Voltaire.
b. Mistress of King Louis XVI.
c. Famous letter writer.
d. Wife of King Louis XIV.

27. Match the word to its closest synonym:

a. Meretricious	**1.** Severe
b. Draconian	**2.** Irregular
c. Taciturn	**3.** Uncommunicative
d. Sententious	**4.** Flashy
e. Tractable	**5.** Pompous
f. Anomalous	**6.** Docile

28. Which of the following states was _not_ part of the Confederacy?

a. Arkansas	**c.** Kentucky
b. Florida	**d.** Texas

29. Mark the following statements _T_ for true or _F_ for false.

a. Plants have sexual organs. ____

b. Sun spots can cause storms on earth. ____

c. More female children are conceived than male. ____

d. Matter is neither created nor destroyed in a chemical reaction. ____

e. Sponges are plants. ____

f. All atoms weigh the same. ____

g. Acquired characteristics can be inherited. ____

h. The earth revolves around the sun, spins on its axis, and wobbles from side to side. ____

SCORING: Give yourself one point for each correct answer:

1. b.   **2. d.**

3. a.5 (Italian), **b.8** (Latin), **c.2** (German), **d.4** (Italian), **e.3** (Latin), **f.7** (German), **g.1** (French), **h.6** (French). Give yourself two extra points if you identified all the languages correctly.

4. a.   **5. d.**   **6. d.**

7. a.4, b.1, c.2, d.5, e.3, f.6

8. b.   **9. a.**   **10. d.**

11. a.6, b.5, c.4, d.2, e.3, f.1   **12. b.**

13. a. (If $\frac{2}{3}x = 40$, then $3 \times \frac{2}{3}x = 3 \times 40$; therefore $\frac{6}{3} x = 120$; $2x = 120$; $x = 60$)

14. d.   **15. a.6, b.1, c.3, d.5, e.2, f.4**

16. c.   **17. d.**   **18. b.**

19. a.3, b.8, c.1, d.7, e.2, f.4, g.10, h.6, i.9, j.5

20. c. (_All for Love_ is by Dryden.)

21. a. (The sequence is plus one, minus two, plus three, minus four, etc.)

22. a.6, b.1, c.5, d.3, e.2, f.4

23. b.   **24. b.**

25. a.4, b.5, c.3, d.6, e.1, f.2   **26. d.**

27. a.4, b.1, c.3, d.5, e.6, f.2   **28. c.**

29. a.T, b.T, c.F, d.T, e.F, f.F, g.F, h.T

YOUR GRADE

A+ (over 78): Congratulations and go to the head of the class. Learning is a natural process for you; you have a good mind and many interests.

A (71 to 78): A very good score! The amount of general knowledge you've acquired is far greater than standard!

B (61 to 70): Above average; you probably did well in school, but since then, you've become rusty on subjects you don't _need_ to know about.

C (46 to 60): Average; you _could_ do better! Try really _reading_ your daily paper . . . you'll be surprised how much interesting information is hiding there!

D (30 to 45): Just barely passing. Did you forget everything you learned . . . or weren't you _really_ paying attention in the first place? Either way, you've still got a chance to learn.

F (under 30): Wherever your head is—up in the clouds or under a mushroom—_learning_ doesn't thrill you. If you really can get along without knowing your world, fine: if not, maybe you should visit your neighborhood library.

The 25-Minute I.Q. Test

HAROLD AND LOUISE BURNSTEIN

Have you ever wondered what your IQ is? This simplified test will tell your score quickly and with reasonable accuracy. Don't start the test until you're sure you won't be interrupted; spend *exactly* twenty-five minutes and then stop. Don't stay too long with any one question. If one stumps you, go on to the next and return to the unanswered one if time allows. Here are four sample questions:

1. *Puppy* **is to** *dog,* **as** *kitten* **is to:**
  a. Fish   **c.** Cat
  b. Animals   **d.** Monkey   (C)

2. In this series, what number comes next?
  4, 6, 8, 10   (12)

3. These words can be arranged to form a sentence. If the sentence is true, write T, if the sentence is false, write F:
  is   always   water   blue   (F)

4. In this group, which object does not belong?
  1. Pencil   **3.** Hammer
  2. Pen   **4.** Crayon   (3.)

Important: You may use a separate sheet of paper for calculating (scoring explained at the end of test).

NOW, START (Time—twenty-five minutes)
1. *Piano* **is to** *play,* **as** *book* **is to:**
  1. Scream   **3.** Dance
  2. Read   **4.** Run   ( )

2. In this series, what number comes next?
  3, 9, 15, 21   ( )

3. These words can be arranged to form a sentence. If the sentence is true, write T. If the sentence is false, write F:
  burn   paper   can   wet   ( )

4. These words can be arranged to form a sentence. If the sentence is true, write T. If the sentence is false, write F:
  on   floats   wood   never   water   ( )

5. In this series, what number comes next? 1, 3, 5, 7   ( )

6. *Cautious* means:
  1. Important   **3.** Careful
  2. Negligent   **4.** Careless   ( )

7. *He* is to *him*, as *she* is to:
  1. Me   **3.** Her
  2. Theirs   **4.** His   ( )

8. In this group, which object does not belong?
  1. Radio   **3.** Football
  2. Clock   **4.** Battery   ( )

9. In this group, which word does not belong?
  1. Builder   **3.** Architect
  2. Bricklayer   **4.** Dentist   ( )

10. In this series, what number comes next?
  33, 44, 55, 66   ( )

11. *Botanist* is to *sociology* as *plant* is to:
  1. Men   **3.** Society
  2. Train   **4.** Headache   ( )

12. In this series, what letter comes next?
  A, C, E, G, I   ( )

13. Which letter does not belong in this series?
  Z, Y, X, B, W, V   ( )

14. Physical education makes for:
  1. Godliness   **3.** Silver
  2. Health   **4.** Skating   ( )

15. ⌐ is to \ as ⌐ is to:
  1. ⊔⊔ **2.** ⟨ **3.** ⊐ **4.** ⟩   ( )

16. A canoe always has:
  1. Paddles   **3.** Water
  2. Canvas   **4.** Length   ( )

17. In this series, what number comes next?
  2, A, 9, B, 6, C, 13, D   ( )

18. Twenty men can dig 40 holes in 60 days, so 10 men can dig 20 holes in how many days?   ( )

19. In this series, which number does not belong?
  2, 4, 100, 38, 20, 7   ( )

20. In this series, which letter comes next?
  A, C, B, D, F, E, G   ( )

21. If all men have shoes, then big men have:
  1. Big shoes   **3.** Shoes
  2. Old shoes   **4.** Green shoes   ( )

22. In this series, what number comes next?
  2, 9, 6, 7, 18, 5   ( )

23. In this group, which word does not belong?
  1. Sadness   **3.** Sorrow
  2. Melancholy   **4.** Mourning   ( )

24. ◉ is to ○ as ■ is to:
  1. □ **2.** ● **3.** ■ **4.** ◨   ( )

25. How many miles can a dog run in 3 minutes if the dog runs half as fast as a car going at the rate of 40 miles per hour?   ( )

26. One series below is in opposite order to

the other, except for a particular number. Write the number.

1, 2, 3   1, 3, 2   ( )

27. In this group, which word does not belong?
1. The   3. An
2. A   4. It   ( )

28. ☐ is to ⊓ as ◇ is to:

1. ⬦   2. ⬡   3. ⬢   4. ⊓   ( )

29. *Plane* is to *solid* as *line* is to:
1. Square   4. Rectangle
2. Circle   5. Plane
3. Angle   ( )

30. In this series, what number comes next?
2, A, 9, B, 6, C, 13, D   ( )

31. *Comprehensible* advice is:
1. Bad   3. Understandable
2. Reprehensible   4. Good   ( )

32. Half a waiter's earnings, and a dollar besides, comes from tips. If he earns 15 dollars, how many dollars come from tips?   ( )

33. Which of these words most nearly corresponds in meaning to *delete*?
1. Sell   3. File
2. Erase   4. Rent   ( )

34. People always have:
1. Fringes   4. Cars
2. Shoes   5. Bodies   (.)
3. Hair

35. *Pique* is most similar in meaning to:
1. Choice   4. Resentment
2. Decoration   5. Sorrow   ( )
3. Dwarf

36. When Carol makes soup, she puts in 1 bean for each 2 peas. If her soup contains a total of 300 peas and beans, how many peas are there?   ( )

37. No cat can sing, but some cats can talk. If so:
1. Some cats can sing.
2. All cats can't sing.
3. All cats can't talk.   ( )

38. Stockings always have:
1. Holes   3. Seams
2. Weight   4. Garters   ( )

39. One bunch of potatoes has one-third again as many potatoes as a second bunch. If the second bunch has 3 fewer potatoes than the first bunch, how many has the first bunch?   ( )

40. Birds can only fly and hop, but worms can crawl; therefore:
1. Birds eat worms.
2. Birds don't crawl.
3. Birds sometimes crawl.   ( )

41. *Bird* is to *fish* as *airplane* is to:
1. Boat   4. Ship
2. Whale   5. Submarine   ( )
3. Dory

42. Boxes always have:
1. Angles   3. Drawers
2. Shapes   4. Covers   ( )

43. George gets twice as large a share of the profits as any of his three partners gets. The three partners share equally. What fraction of the entire profits is George's?   ( )

44. What number is as much more than 10 as it is less than one-half of what 30 is 10 less than?   ( )

45. These words can be arranged to form a sentence. If the sentence is true, write T. If the sentence is false, write F.

one	in	is	number
than	more	cars	car ( )

SCORING: 1 (2), 2 (27), 3 (F), 4 (F), 5 (9), 6 (3), 7 (3), 8 (3), 9 (4), 10 (77), 11 (3), 12 (K), 13 (B), 14 (2), 15 (3), 16 (4), 17 (10), 18 (60), 19 (7), 20 (I), 21 (3), 22 (54), 23 (4), 24 (3), 25 (1), 26 (1), 27 (4), 28 (3), 29 (5), 30 (10), 31 (3), 32 (8½), 33 (2), 34 (5), 35 (4), 36 (200), 37 (2), 38 (2), 39 (12), 40 (2), 41 (5), 42 (2), 43 (⅖), 44 (15), 45 (F).

Table of Mental Ages (in Months)

your score	your mental age	your score	your mental age
2	94	11	113
3	96	12	115
4	98	13	117
5	100	14	119
6	103	15	122
7	105	16	124
8	107	17	126
9	109	18	128
10	111	19	130
20	132	55	206
21	134	56	208
22	136	57	210
23	138	58	212
24	140	59	214
25	143	60	216
26	145	61	218
27	147	62	221
28	149	63	223
29	151	64	225
30	153	65	227
31	155	66	229
32	157	67	231
33	159	68	233
34	162	69	235
35	164	70	237
36	166	71	240
37	168	72	242
38	170	73	244
39	172	74	246
40	174	75	248
41	176	76	250
42	178	77	252
43	181	78	254
44	183	79	256
45	185	80	259
46	187	81	261
47	189	82	263
48	191	83	265
49	193	84	267
50	195	85	269
51	197	86	271
52	199	87	273
53	202	88	275
54	204	89	278

FIGURING YOUR IQ: In order to find your IQ after taking the test, proceed as follows:
1. For each correct answer, score 2 points.
2. By examining the table on this page, locate the Mental Age equivalent to your test score.

Are You Truly A Gourmet?

CHRISTOPHER IRBY

Yyou're at the *Tour d' Argent* in Paris, dining with Julia Child, Craig Claiborne, and James Beard. (Don't ask how you got there, just play the game!) To impress them as a woman of sophistication and experience, you really should know your *aioli* from your *entrecôte*, your 1959 *Chateau Lafitte* from your 1969 *Chablis*. Will you measure up? Why not grab a pencil and find out . . .

1. Hmm, there's something odd about the *Sauce Béarnaise*. Which ingredient does *not* belong?
a. Tarragon
b. Butter
c. Shallots
d. Rosemary
e. Vinegar
f. Egg yolks

2. The best way to store wine is:

a.   **b.**   **c.**

3. Regardless of your personal tastes, which of the following is generally considered to be the most "peasanty" meat?
a. Beef
b. Pork
c. Chicken
d. Veal
e. Lamb
f. Fish

4. You'd eat *blini* with:
a. Green mayonnaise
b. Caviar
c. Whipped cream

5. Here's a list of well-known European wines. Put an *R* next to each red, a *W* next to each white:
a. Liebfraumilch
b. Chianti
c. Haut-Médoc
d. Pommard
e. Soave
f. Moselle
g. Bardolino
h. Chablis
i. Châteauneuf du-Pape
j. Pouilly-Fuissé

6. In Vienna, you order *Wiener Schnitzel* because you have a craving for:
a. Frankfurters and sauerkraut
b. Stuffed cabbage leaves
c. Stewed beef with noodles
d. Breaded veal cutlets

7. Match the cooking style with its distinguishing ingredients:

a. Creole

b. Florentine

c. Provençale

d. Bourguignonne

e. Romana

f. Bolognese

1. Red wine, small whole onions, mushroom caps
2. Ground meat, tomato sauce
3. Tabasco, green peppers, onions, tomatoes
4. Garlic, olive oil, tomatoes, Mediterranean herbs
5. Spinach
6. Butter, cream or egg yolks, cheese

8. In which glass would you serve champagne?

a.   b.

9. Which cheeses from the right-hand column could be substituted for those on the left in a culinary clinch?

a. Ricotta

b. Gruyère

c. Edam

d. Gorgonzola

e. Port salut

f. Romano

1. Bel Paese
2. Blue cheese
3. Parmesan
4. Swiss cheese
5. Cottage cheese
6. Gouda

10. A recipe for a classic Beef Wellington would include (choose four):

a. Carrots and onions
b. Dijon mustard
c. Pastry crust
d. Madeira
e. Pâté de foie gras
f. Demi-glace sauce
g. Artichoke bottoms
h. Truffles

11. Match the California varietal wine with the appropriate European wine "type":

a. Pinot Noir

b. Sylvaner

c. Cabernet Sauvignon

d. Gamay

e. Pinot Chardonnay

f. Sémillon

1. Beaujolais
2. White Bordeaux
3. Rhine wine
4. Red Burgundy
5. Red Bordeaux
6. White Burgundy

12. At a formal dinner prepared by a great chef, you wouldn't expect to see _____ on the table:

a. Fish forks

b. Salt and pepper

c. Finger bowls

d. Water glasses

13. The paper frills used to decorate the bony ends of lamb chops and *supremes* of chicken are called:

a. Coronets

b. Serviettes

c. Collars

d. Papillotes

14. Match courses on this menu (listed below in order from *a* to *f*) with the wines and spirits that best complement them:

a. Fresh caviar

b. Striped bass with champagne sauce

c. Stuffed squabs (with braised endive, watercress, Boston lettuce salad)

d. Brie

e. Grapefruit sherbert

f. Coffee

1. Montrachet (white Burgundy)
2. Vodka
3. Dom Pérignon (champagne)
4. Cognac
5. Chateau Ausone (red Bordeaux)
6. Romanée-Conti (red Burgundy)

15. Herb or spice? Indicate the appropriate classification with an *H* or an *S*.

a. Anise

b. Sage

c. Marjoram
d. Caraway
e. Bay leaves
f. Mace

g. Cloves
h. Fennel
i. Mustard
j. Savory

16. Each dish on the left typifies of the "schools" of Chinese cooking on the right. Pair them up:
a. Chow mein
b. Peking duck
c. Chicken with hot peppers
d. Sweet and sour fish

1. Szechwan
2. Cantonese
3. Hunan
4. Mandarin

17. In planning a dinner party, you might consider serving which of the following as *hors d'oeuvre* (you may choose more than one):
a. Guacamole
b. Stuffed eggs
c. Rumaki
d. Canapés Camille
e. Steak Tartare

f. Rollmops
g. Spiedini
h. Pastels
i. All of the above

18. Can you match these delicacies with their descriptions?
a. Dolmas
b. Gazpacho
c. Sashimi
d. Coquilles Saint-Jacques
e. Braciole
f. Osso Buco

1. Rolled beef in tomato sauce
2. Baked scallops
3. Stuffed grape leaves
4. Braised veal knuckles
5. Sliced raw fish
6. Chilled vegetable soup

19. At an elegant international restaurant, you'd refer to the wine steward as the:
a. Maitre d'hôtel
b. Garçon

c. Sommelier
d. Tastevin

20. Match the dessert with the topping traditionally served with it:
a. Coffee Charlotte russe
b. Plum pudding
c. Chocolate soufflé
d. Peach melba
e. Strawberry Chantilly
f. Biscuit tortoni
1. Whipped cream
2. Confectioner's sugar
3. Shaved chocolate
4. Macaroon crumbs
5. Raspberry purée
6. Hard sauce

SCORING: Give yourself one point for each correct answer.

1. d.
2. a. This keeps the cork moist enough that it won't crumble when you pull it out, or shrink, allowing air to enter and ruin the wine. Also, storing wine diagonally prevents the sediment which forms at the bottom of older reds from becoming churned up when you right the bottle for opening. If your space is limited, however, "B," the next best method, may be the easiest to manage.
3. b. Hearty, greasy, and bland, pork is seldom included in the highest of *haute cuisine*.
4. b. What else? And of course you wouldn't forget to top these Russian buckwheat pancakes with sour cream.
5. a.W, b.R, c.R, d.R, e.W, f.W, g.R, h.W, i.R, j.W
6. d.
7. a.3, b.5, c.4, d.1, e.6, f.2
8. b. The tulip shape collects and "holds" *any* wine's bouquet, or aroma. And with cham-

pagne, it also keeps those lovely bubbles from fizzling out into the air, where *you* can't enjoy them.

9. a.5, b.4, c.5, d.2, e.1, f.3

10. a. c. e. h.

11. a.4, b.3, c.5, d.1, e.6, f.2

12. b. They've already been used by the chef with such perfection that you won't need them —indeed, to ask for them would be an unpardonable insult!

13. d.

14. a.2, b.1, c.5, d.6, e.3, f.4. Here's why: Caviar with straight vodka is a Russian custom (but you'd take it easy, of course, since you wouldn't want this potent drink to dull your tastebuds). In order to appreciate the subtleties of each wine, you'd drink them from "lightest" to "fullest." Whites are more delicate than reds, so you'd have the Montrachet first, then, because red Bordeaux is never as robust and hearty as red Burgundy, the Ausone, and finally the Romanée. Although you *could* serve champagne with any course, it's the only wine on this list that's appropriate with dessert. Coffee with brandy is traditional.

15. a.S, b.H, c.H, d.S, e.H, f.S, g.S, h.H, i.S, j.H. Herbs are leafy; spices seedy or woody, like fennel seed and cinnamon bark.

16. a.2, b.4, c.1, d.3

17. They're all *hors d'oeuvre,* so give yourself 8 points for "i" or one point for each other letter. Mystified by these exotic items? Guacamole, in case you need enlightening, is spicy Mexican avocado paste, while Japanese rumaki are roasted, marinated chicken livers, water chestnuts, and bacon sprinkled with brown sugar. To make canapés camilles as the French do, spread a circle of toast with mustard, butter, and purée of beef tongue and chicken livers. Steak tartare, another French favorite, is raw chopped beef seasoned with herbs, spices, and sometimes raw egg, while rollmops, a Yiddish treat, is rolled, marinated herring, stuffed with onions. Spiedini is toasted Italian bread topped with grill mozzarella and an anchovy. And finally, pastels —which come from Morocco—are delicate pastry shells filled with grilled, chopped lamb or beef. There now, doesn't that make you hungry?

18. a.3, b.6, c.5, d.2, e.1, f.4

19. c. The Maître d'hôtel is the headwaiter, or in elegant American restaurants, the "Captain." (The true gourmet *never* says "Maître d'!" The "garçon" is what you'd call your waiter, and a *tastevin* is the small, metal wine-tasting cup the sommelier wears on a chain around his neck.

20. a.3, b.6, c.2, d.5, e.1, f.4

YOUR RATING

81 points: *Cordon Bleu.* With this perfect score, you're not only a bonafide gourmet, but also an oenophile *par excellence!*

65-80: *Cordon Rouge.* Another Julia Child you aren't, but someday you *might* be.

40-64: *Honorable Mention.* Not bad. Now all you need to improve your expertise is a wider range of experience.

39 and under: *Culinary Klutz.* Sure you've got consuming passions—but they're not wining and dining!

So You Think You Know Nutrition!

C. K. NICHOLAS

Food—it can please you, charm you, buoy you up, and keep you as healthy as a race horse . . . or it can glut you, cause exhaustion, and make you sickly and depressed! Do you *know* how to eat right for satisfying, glorious health? Take our quiz and find out.

1. One of the following breakfasts is best for all-round nutrition and day-long well-being. Which?
a. Fresh-fruit salad, bran muffin, decaffeinated coffee
b. Grapefruit slices, whole-wheat cereal with milk, tea or coffee
c. Fruit juice, one egg, one-half cup cottage cheese, crisp bacon, tea or coffee
d. Fruit juice, three scrambled eggs, one-half piece toast, tea or coffee

2. This first meal of the day is particularly important because:
a. A good breakfast will establish stable energy production throughout the day, without severe highs or lows.
b. Breakfast should account for 25 percent of the day's nutritional needs.
c. High-protein foods taken in morning keep blood sugar up longer than any other.
d. Your body needs a high proportion of nutrients after a night's fast.

3. Three of the following statements about fats are true. Which one is not?
a. Fat is crucial for body functioning.

b. It's digested at a slower rate to keep you hunger-free longer.
c. Fat has fewer calories (per ounce) than sugar.
d. There are two forms: hard fat (found in meat), soft fat (found in seafood).

4. When you cook with oil, you'll want to choose any but *one* of the following oils because *it* is less nutritious. Which?
a. Olive oil
c. Cottonseed oil
b. Corn oil
d. Peanut oil

5. A heavy smoker should increase the intake of *one* of these vitamins that the body doesn't retain as well as it does in nonsmokers. Which?
a. Vitamin A
c. Vitamin B complex
b. Vitamin C
d. Vitamin D

6. Many nutritionists now agree that of the following fruits, the one with the all-around *best* nutritional value is the:
a. Orange
d. Banana
b. Apple
e. Cantaloupe
c. Grapefruit

7. Drinking one of these beverages before dinner will stimulate your appetite to help digestion. Which one?
a. Coffee
c. Wine
b. Low-calorie soda
d. Grapefruit juice

8. If you have the following symptoms— "goose-pimpling" of the skin, lusterless, dry hair, eye fatigue—suspect a deficiency in:
a. Vitamin B complex
c. Niacin
b. Vitamin A
d. Trace minerals

9. Food can be a natural tranquilizer. Which two of the following foods, eaten for lunch or dinner, could make a noticeably calmer you?
a. Asparagus
c. Milk
b. Spinach
d. Calf's liver

10. Adelle Davis, Dr. Roger J. Williams, and Gayelord Hauser are known for:

a. Advocating vegetarian diets
b. Insisting that dietary deficiencies are a primary cause of much disease
c. Food faddism
d. Advising megadoses of vitamins to cure ailments

11. If you decide to take a little vitamin therapy on your own (you read that a massive amount of a certain vitamin would clear your skin, for example), do *not* overdo two of the following vitamins. They must never be taken without first checking the safe daily-allowance dosage. Which two?
a. Vitamin B_1
c. Vitamin E
b. Vitamin A
d. Vitamin D

12. The total number of calories you consume daily makes the difference in whether or not you gain/lose weight. So, if you stayed within your caloric-intake level, you could eat just steak or nothing but pecan pie without influencing your weight. Is this:
a. True
b. False

13. Brown sugar, raw sugar, and molasses contain calcium and iron. Refined white sugar provides *nothing* but calories. Is this:
a. True
b. False

14. The normally active woman needs at least 60 grams of protein each day. Which one of the following lunches would provide *half* her protein needs?
a. One-quarter pound hamburger, scoop of cottage cheese, a slice of tomato, coffee
b. Chicken salad, a glass of milk, a fresh peach
c. Two eggs, two slices of ham, a green salad, tea
d. Yogurt with two tablespoons wheat germ, apple, coffee

15. If you go on a *low*-carbohydrate diet, you'd avoid two of the following vegetables. Two others are acceptable in your diet. Which ones?

a. Beets   **c.** Lima beans
b. Corn   **d.** Carrots

SCORING:

1. c. It is both highest in protein and the best *source* of protein. Breakfast **d.** is *not* an ideal protein vehicle because eggs contain considerable amounts of cholesterol.

2. c. Since protein is a slow-burning energy source, it's good to start the day with a plentiful supply of it. Statements **a., b.,** and **d.** are *not* correct.

3. c. Is incorrect. Fat contains the *most* calories per ounce.

4. a. Olive oil does not contain as many of the essential fatty acids as the other oils do.

5. b. Vitamin C will not necessarily guard against the harmful effects of tobacco, but as a smoker you need more than the normal daily intake.

6. e. Cantaloupe contains significant amounts of Vitamin A plus almost as much Vitamin C as an orange, so on balance it is the most nutritious. Bananas and apples have much smaller quantities of these two important vitamins.

7. c. Wine, in moderate amounts, stimulates the flow of gastric juices and promotes efficient digestion.

8. b. Vitamin A is particularly important for good skin, hair, and eyesight.

9. a. and **c.** They're rich in calcium.

10. b. The three writers named have long been known for saying that unrecognized, subclinical diet deficiencies are responsible for many common ailments.

11. b. and **d.** Vitamins A and D can both be toxic in large doses.

12. a. True, but for optimum health we need a diet rich in *all* the essential nutriments.

13. a. True, but most authorities recommend getting your iron and calcium from sources other than sugar or molasses.

14. a. Would be best (33 grams of protein). Lunches **a., b.,** and **d.** also contain protein but *not* that much.

15. a. and **d.** Corn and lima beans would be too starchy and high in calories for you.

Give yourself three points for every correctly answered question. For multiple answer questions 9, 11, and 15 score three points for *each* right answer.

45-54: Congratulations, you qualify as a nutritional *scholar*. You know the food value of just about everything, so now please make sure you eat *right!*

33-42: Your grasp of nutrition is good. Occasionally you probably consume (by mistake, of course) foods that are overly fattening or full of "empty" calories, but most of the time you're able to choose the very best of meals.

18-30: Yes, you do know *something* about what's healthy to eat . . . but we advise you to down a good vitamin and mineral capsule to make up for what you *don't!*

Below 18: Rush to the nearest bookstore and get yourself a copy of Adelle Davis's *Let's Eat Right to Keep Fit!*

Test Your Trivia

BILL SLATTERY

Have you ever considered that being a trivia mavin isn't a *trivial* accomplishment but something to be extraordinarily proud of? Not only does your encyclopedic recall reveal a passion for knowledge, but an unquenchable curiosity about *literally* everything in the world. Curious to discover just how inquiring and retentive your mind is? Then lock up all your reference books, resist the impulse to call friends for help, and take our little quiz to find out how much you really *do* know . . .

1. Jim Bouton, Arthur Godfrey, Dean Martin, and Abbie Hoffman have this in common:
a. They're ace pilots.
b. They've had vasectomies.
c. They were football team captains in high school.
d. They're expert photographers.
e. Pisces is their zodiac sign.

2. Ann-Margret, Eydie Gormé, Lana Turner, Dinah Shore, and Raquel Welch all share this interest or experience:
a. These female stars fancy felines.
b. In high school, they were cheerleaders.
c. As kids, they wore braces.
d. California is their native state.
e. They've all been romanced by Burt Reynolds.

3. The first female U.S. presidential candidate was . . .

a. Amelia Jenks Bloomer.
b. Susan B. Anthony.
c. Elizabeth Stanton.
d. Isabella Hooker.
e. Victoria Claflin Woodhull.

4. Who said, "If I'm not there, start without me"?
a. Tallulah Bankhead d. Texas Guinan
b. Cole Porter e. Admiral Farragut
c. George M. Cohan

5. The world's tiniest country is . . .
a. Liechtenstein. d. Seychelles.
b. Malta. e. Monaco.
c. Andorra.

6. In the left-hand column are recently coined words and phrases. Match them with their proper meanings in the right-hand column.

1. Blinger a. A musical arrangement
2. Plain wrapper b. Rapid eye movement during dreams
3. REM
4. Deep-six c. An unmarked police car
5. Chart d. To discard
  e. Big, huge

7. Match these female superstars with their real names:
1. Ava Gardner a. Doris Von Kappelhoff
2. Lauren Bacall b. Dianne Bellmont
3. Lucille Ball c. Betty Perske
4. Doris Day d. Lucy Johnson
5. Judy Garland e. Frances Gumm

8. "Able was I ere I saw Elba" is a famous . . .
a. Metaphor. d. Zeugma.
b. Palindrome. e. Simile.
c. Oxymoron.

9. Fang, Fon, Fulani, Twi, and Oriya are *all* names of . . .
a. Snakes d. Birds
b. Languages e. Rivers
c. Mammals

10. Napoleon and Josephine were both married twice. True or false?

11. In the left-hand column below is a list of dates. The right-hand column consists of an important historical event or person associated with one of these dates. Try to match.
1. 1066 a. A monarch's death
2. 1901 b. The name of a famous novel
3. 1899 c. An important event for author Ernest Hemingway
4. 1789 d. The start of a bloody revolution
5. 1984 e. A famous conquest

12. In 1975, how did Sandra Palmer win $180,000?
a. In a lottery d. At Forest Hills
b. Playing golf e. Wrestling
c. In the Daytona 500

13. Nicky Hilton, Michael Wilding, Mike Todd, Eddie Fisher, Richard Burton, and John Warner have all been married to Elizabeth Taylor. How many times has Miss Taylor been married and divorced? _____

14. In ancient Egypt, women used a donkey's hoof soaked in oil as a . . .
a. Pomade. d. Rouge.
b. Hair restorer. e. Depilatory.
c. Makeup remover.

15. The late Israeli prime minister Golda Meir was born in . . . d. Russia.
a. Milwaukee, Wisconsin. e. Poland.
b. Israel.
c. New York City.

16. What is the highest price *ever* paid for dinner for two?
a. $300 b. $500 c. $1,000
d. $2,000 e. $4,000

17. For many years, Eleanor Roosevelt wrote a daily column that ran in many newspapers. It was called . . .
a. "My Day." **d.** "New Times."
b. "Your Day." **e.** "Mrs. Roosevelt Says."
c. "Our Times."

18. In an average day, how many Coca-Colas are sold?
a. 1.85 million **d.** 1.85 billion
b. 18.5 million **e.** 18.5 billion
c. 185 million

19. According to the *Guinness Book of World Records*, the most versatile athlete in the world was a woman. (Versatility here means a champion athlete in many sports—golf, swimming, tennis, etc.) She was . . .
a. Linda Ellerbee. **d.** Billie Jean King.
b. Chris Evert. **e.** Babe Didrikson Zaharias.
c. Diana Nyad.

20. The largest airline in the world is:
a. Pan American. **b.** United. **c.** Air India.
d. Aeroflot. **e.** People's Airline of China.

21. In proportion to its size, which male animal or insect has the longest sexual organ?
a. Horse **b.** Man **c.** Flea
d. Elephant **e.** Mosquito

22. Which one of the following creatures makes love the longest in one session?
a. Dog **b.** Flea **c.** Man
d. Waterbug **e.** Shetland pony

23. For your birthday, you want your lover to buy you the *most* expensive stone. Which would he choose?
a. Chrysoberyl **d.** Spinel
b. Corundum **e.** Peridot
c. Aquamarine

1. 2. 3. 4.

24. Pictured above are four actresses. Match names to photos.
a. Mariette Hartley **c.** Margaret Hamilton
b. Valerie Bertinelli **d.** Zohra Lampert

1. 2. 3. 4.

25. Above are photographs of four actors. Again, match names with pictures.
a. Marc Lawrence **c.** Murray Hamilton
b. Elisha Cook, Jr. **d.** Fritz Weaver

SCORING: **Give yourself 4 points for each correct answer:**

1. b.

2. b.

3. e. Victorian suffragist Victoria Woodhull ran against President Ulysses S. Grant in 1872. Her platform included short skirts, free love, legalized prostitution, and tax reform. Though Victoria was in jail on election day, charged with sending "obscenity" through the mail, she won a few thousand votes anyway.

4. a. Tallulah Bankhead made this remark to a man who propositioned her.

5. e. Monaco—a country on the Mediterranean coast of France—is just slightly larger than one-half square mile.

6. 1.e, 2.c, 3.b, 4.d, 5.a

7. 1.d, 2.c, 3.b, 4.a, 5.e

8. b. A *palindrome* is a verse, sentence, word (as *madam*), or a number (1881) that reads the same forward as backward. A *metaphor* is a literally untrue comparison as in, "He is a river to his people." *Oxymoron* is a combination of two incongruous words—e.g., *thunderous silence* or *sweet sorrow*. *Zeugma* is a figure of speech in which a verb or adjective applies to two or more words, but logically connects to only one, as in "She went white and out the door." A *simile,* like a metaphor, compares two dissimilar things, but must have the word *like* or *as* in it; for example, "She is like a rose."

9. b. Fang, Fon, Fulani and Twi are names of African languages. Oriya is spoken by some 20 million people in northern India.

10. True. Josephine was a widow—her first husband, Viscount de Beauharnais, lost his head during the French Revolution. When the beautiful Creole failed to produce an heir to the throne, Napoleon divorced her and married Marie-Louise, Archduchess of Austria, who bore him a son the following year.

11. **1.e, 2.a, 3.c, 4.d, 5.b.** The Norman Conquest of England was completed in 1066. Doughty Queen Victoria died in 1901 after ruling Britain for sixty-four years. Nobel-prize-winning novelist Ernest Hemingway was born in 1899. The French Revolution began in 1789; and *1984* is the title of a terrifying novel about the future written by British author George Orwell.

12. b. Sandra Palmer, who turned pro golfer in 1974, won the Dinah Shore Open the following year.

13. Elizabeth Taylor has been married *seven* times—twice to Richard Burton—and divorced *five* times, though not from producer Mike Todd, who died in a plane crash in 1958.

14. b. This *asinine* remedy, Egyptian ladies believed, would grow luxuriant tresses on bald scalps.

15. d. Though Golda Meir grew up in Milwaukee, Wisconsin, she was born in 1898 in Kiev, Russia.

16. e. At a quiet dinner for two at Chez Denis in Paris, gourmets Craig Claiborne and Pierre Franey consumed a grand total of thirty-one dishes—including fresh Beluga caviar, three soups, a chartreuse of partridge, several pastries—and nine wines. Cost: $4,000, a tab picked up by American Express which had donated the dinner at a 1975 TV fund-raising auction. After this sumptuous repast, the gourmands—feeling like Henry VIII, Gargantua, Lucullus, and Bacchus all rolled into one—somehow managed to get up from the table.

17. a. "My Day" was started in 1936 and ran for almost thirty years.

18. c

19. e. Babe Didrikson Zaharias, who died in 1956, set new records at the 1932 Olympics in the javelin throw, eighty-meter hurdles, and high-jump; from 1940 to 1950, she won every golf title including World and National Open. Incredibly versatile Babe also excelled at billiards, basketball, figure skating, diving, lacrosse, baseball and was, in fact, exceptional at every sport she tried except Ping-Pong.

20. d. Aeroflot is the world's largest airline. United is second, followed by Pan Am and Air India. There is no People's Airline of China.

21. c. The male flea's sexual organ is triple the rest of its body in length.

22. d. Waterbugs have been observed having intercourse for as long as two weeks nonstop!

23. b. The corundum is the only precious jewel on the list; the rest are semiprecious. Pure, transparent varieties of this mineral—second only to the diamond in hardness—include the ruby and sapphire.

24. 1-c, 2-d, 3-b, 4-a
25. 1-b, 2-d, 3-a, 4-c,

HOW YOU RATE

Over 140: Your knowledge of current affairs and world history is superb; throw out your old encyclopedias and almanacs and start writing the revised editions yourself!

100 to 140 points: Your informational grasp is excellent. Possibly you were on "Quiz Kid" as a child. At parties, you can always be counted on to keep the conversation flowing and lively.

60 to 100 points: Do you listen to a lot of disco music instead of reading? Try visiting the library occasionally and browsing through the reference books. You'll be surprised to discover how much fun it is to learn fascinating facts about many different subjects.

Below 60 points: Subscribe to several magazines and newspapers, read them regularly: soon you'll be able to perk up your conversation with tantalizingly informative tidbits that will command your man's attention as much as that fetching smile!

Test Your Economic Acumen

SUSAN KRUG FRIEDMAN

Our 1980s economy is *tricky,* and the days when you could afford to be *blasé* about complicated fiscal matters are over. Smart ladies know their very survival can depend on a grasp of financial phenomena, while lazy-minded girls who think economics are just too boring stay ignorant at their *peril!* Understanding how money works, though not always easy, is *important* . . . so to find out how far *you* have to go, take this little quiz. (Don't feel too terrible if you flunk . . . terms used by economists sound formidable, but you can educate yourself with a little diligent reading. *The Money Book,* by Sylvia Porter, published by Doubleday, is a fine primer for a girl who wants to *sharpen* economic savvy.)

1. GNP is:
a. One of the 500 largest U.S. firms.
b. The value of all goods and services produced in the economy.
c. A measure of stock-market activity.

2. The Consumer Price Index measures:
a. The change in prices of a "typical" family's purchases.
b. The cost of necessities.
c. Wholesale prices

3. Petrodollars refers to:
a. Profits earned by U.S. oil companies.
b. U.S. dollars held by oil-rich nations.

c. Earnings from off-shore drilling.
d. Revenues from gasoline excise taxes.

4. The Federal Reserve System:
a. Provides loans to small businesses.
b. Is an affiliation of the twenty-five largest U.S. banks.
c. Was established as a lender of last resort for banks.

5. The situation of declining output and employment accompanied by rising prices is called:
a. Depression   c. Inflation
b. Recession   d. Stagflation

6. Opportunity cost is:
a. The potential value of any activity that is forgone when you choose an alternative activity.
b. The cost involved in creating opportunities for labor.
c. The cost of entering a new field.

7. Corporations with operations in foreign countries are known as:
a. Monopolies
b. Oligopolies
c. Multinationals
d. Conglomerates

8. Changes in government taxation and spending are examples of:
a. Discount policy
b. Monetary policy
c. Fiscal policy
d. Open-market operations

9. If a corporation fails, which of these investors will be paid first? second? last?
a. Owners of common stock
b. Owners of bonds
c. Owners of preferred stock

10. The holder of a bond receives ____; the bond represents ____ of the corporation.
a. Dividends, ownership
b. Interest, a debt
c. Dividends, a debt
d. Interest, ownership

11. The idea that citizens are resources in which society should invest is:
a. Socialism
b. Human capital
c. Egalitarianism

12. When the flow of money out of the country is greater than the inflow of money from abroad, there is:
a. A deficit in the balance of payments.
b. A surplus in the balance of payments.
c. A surplus in the balance of trade.

13. Lowering the value of a nation's currency relative to that of other nations is called:
a. Depreciation
b. Deficit financing
c. Devaluation
d. Deflation

14. You can have a checking account at all:
a. Commercial banks
b. Savings and loan associations
c. Both

15. Regular passbook savings accounts can legally earn higher rates of interest at:
a. Savings and loan associations
b. Commercial banks
c. The legal interest-rate ceilings are the same.

16. Savings and loan associations primarily finance:
a. Purchases of new cars.
b. Loans for education.
c. Small loans for personal expenses.
d. Mortgages.

17. A bear market is one in which:
a. Stock prices are depressed.
b. Stock prices are rising.
c. Commodities are scarce.

18. The Dow Jones average:
a. Is an index of all stock prices.
b. Is an index of selected stock prices.
c. Is an index of industrial profits.

19. A mutual fund:
a. Is another name for a conglomerate.
b. Holds stock in many corporations.
c. Is a type of insurance company.

20. A stock broker is paid commission:
a. Only when stocks are sold.
b. Only when stocks are sold for a profit.
c. Only when stocks are purchased.
d. Whenever stocks are bought or sold.

ANSWERS:
1. b. GNP, or the Gross National Product, is the value of the economy's total economic output, measured in dollars: it's generally considered a key indicator of fiscal health.
2. a. The CPI, compiled by the U.S. Department of Labor, shows price changes in a variety of goods, typically purchased by the average, middle-income family. Considered an important indicator of *inflation*.
3. b. Petrodollars are held by oil-rich nations, such as Iran and Saudi Arabia. These countries are now *so* rich that there's much speculation about what they'll do with all their U.S. money!
4. c. The Federal Reserve System is the "banker's bank"—it supervises how *your* bank handles its money, and, should a particular bank fail, guarantees the depositor doesn't lose money.
5. d. Stagflation is a deadly combination of inflation *and* recession. In the past, inflation (rising prices) was generally accompanied by high employment and economic growth, while recession meant lower prices along with falling employment rates. Stagflation combines the less desirable features of both conditions: Not only do we have fewer people working and less economic growth, but prices are *higher!*

6. a. When your work schedule prevents you from undertaking other *potentially* profitable activities, you are paying an opportunity cost. Two hours spent commuting means two hours less that could conceivably have been devoted to a second job or to working on a worthwhile money-making invention.
7. c. A *monopoly* is the *only* firm supplying one particular set of goods or services; an *oligopoly* is one of few suppliers: a *conglomerate* is a firm resulting from a merger of several companies with different products. Any of these corporations may start producing or selling abroad and thus become *multinational*.
8. c. Fiscal policy governs changes in government income and spending; unlike people, a government can spend more than it earns and not lose its credit rating!
9. The owners of bonds **(b)** are paid first; next comes **(c)** owners of preferred stock, and, if any money is left **(a),** owners of common stock, are paid.
10. b. Bondholders are creditors of a corporation, and they receive interest on the debt of a corporation. Share holders are part owners of a corporation, and earn dividends, which are a share of corporate earnings.
11. b. You may not think of yourself as a resource but the government does. The public expense of educating and training a citizen is expected to "pay off" when this person becomes a contributing member of the labor force.
12. a. A deficit in the balance of payments occurs when U.S. citizens spend more money out of the country than non-nationals spend *here*.
13. c. Devaluation is a ploy governments use to try to attract more spending on the part of foreigners. For example, when we devalue the dollar it becomes relatively less "expensive"

than francs, or yen, or other foreign currencies; this means a non-national gets greater value for his money here, and so is encouraged to spend more. Devaluation also encourages *us* to spend money at home; the less our dollar is worth, the less it buys overseas.

14. a. Savings banks don't offer checking accounts.

15. a. You get about .25 percent more interest at a savings bank.

16. d. Savings and loan corporations provide mortgages and are permitted by law to give depositors higher interest rates than commercial banks. (You can't apply to savings and loan banks for personal loans, nor, in most states, can you draw checks on one of their accounts.)

17. a. The market is said to be bearish when stock prices fall, bullish when they're rising.

18. b. Actually, Dow Jones computes several kinds of stock averages, but the best known is the Dow Jones industrials average, an index to the prices of thirty high-quality, blue-chip stocks.

19. b. When you buy into a mutual fund, you are purchasing shares in a variety of companies, instead of putting all your money in a single stock. Mutual funds offer the investor greatest security, but chances of a "big win" are minimized.

20. d. Brokerage fees are based on the total amounts of money transacted: this means your broker makes money when you sell or buy securities even if *you* don't make any.

SCORING: Give yourself 5 points for each correct answer.

100: Smart girl! You know all you *should* about money . . . if you put all that knowledge into action, you'll never have to worry about being poor.

85-95: You've a much better than average understanding of fiscal phenomena, and are probably careful and smart about how you handle your own money.

65-80: Your economic acumen is solidly *average*—you understand the basics but fine points tend to baffle you. A little study wouldn't hurt, and might give you a better grasp of personal finances, too.

Below 60: You need help! Okay, so you don't find economics fascinating—still, you should realize money matters and that people who don't understand cash usually don't have much of it. Start a course of remedial study right away—you may be surprised to find out finance really isn't as mystifying or boring as you've always thought!